Beautiful Beading

A BEGINNER'S GUIDE

D0474241

RUTH WILSON

SALLY MILNER PUBLISHING

First published in 1995 by
Sally Milner Publishing Pty Ltd
PO Box 2104
Bowral NSW 2576
Australia.

©Ruth Wilson 1995

Reprinted 1996, 1999

Diagrams by Jacqui Quennell
Cover photography by Craig Cranko
Inside pages photography by Andrew Elton
Styling by Mary-Anne Danaher
Author photograph by Reg Bennett
Colour separation in Australia by Sphere Color Graphics
Printed in Australia by Impact Printing

National Library of Australia
Cataloguing-in-Publication data:

Wilson, Ruth (Ruth Eleanor).
    Beautiful Beading.

    ISBN 1 86351 147 4.

    1. Beadwork. 2. Dress accessories. 3. Jewelry making..
    I. Title. (Series : Milner craft series).

745.582

CONTENTS

ACKNOWLEDGEMENTS

Thank you to Jacqui Quennell, whose expertise with a computer and endless patience helped prepare this manuscript; to Kerry Strom, my good friend, for her constant encouragement and hours of proof reading; to Sylvia McCann, for supplying beads, fabrics, and for introducing me to teaching; to my students, for without you there would not be a need to design and create new and interesting projects.

Thank you to Nancy and Reg Bennett, Lillian Poon, Kay Langworthy and Amanda Roots for their help and support.

Thank you to my father, Max Langworthy, whose beautiful wooden boxes were made especially for my little fish; to my teacher and friend, Maisie Jarratt, who shared her skill and love of beading with me and always encouraged me to do my own designs – I hope it will give her pleasure to see a student following in her footsteps. The Lord has given us both a gift we want to share with you.

And thank you to my husband, Ray and our children, Naomi, David and Alisha, for without their patience, tolerance and love I could not have written this book.

INTRODUCTION

Beads have fascinated mankind for centuries and they have been used as currency, as a method of counting and, of course, for adornment. Some of the earliest beads discovered were made by stone-age man, who used anything he could find, ranging from shells, beetle wings and dry seed pods, to fish scales. Even small bird bones were threaded onto strips of leather or vine.

Eventually man began attaching them to clothing. Many early 17th century portraits show beaded collars, cuffs and bodices. Even gloves! During the 1920s, beaded dresses, evening purses, hats, shawls and coats were the height of fashion. Some examples of these garments may be seen at the Powerhouse Museum, Darling Harbour, in Sydney.

Beads come in an amazing range of colours, sizes and shapes and are part of the cultural heritage of many countries. Some European countries still have village women threading beads in the same way as they have done for centuries.

There are many ways of attaching beads to fabric, from a simple backstitch, couching, running stitch and whip stitch, to using a tambour hook and frame.

The stitches used in this book are mostly the French embroidery method but, as a lover of all bead work, I have included other methods. All are explained in step-by-step instructions for the beginner. If you follow the instructions carefully, you will be able to create each of the items exactly as shown and, with a little imagination, you will be able to use the stitches to create your own designs.

CHAPTER ONE

MATERIALS

BEADS

SEED BEADS
Seed beads are small, round or shaped beads and can be made from many substances. The most commonly used are made from glass or plastic but you can also get them in wood, metal, pearl, jet, etc.

The sizes and shapes of seed beads vary greatly and can be very confusing for the beginner. I have tried to simplify things to give you a basic understanding of what to look for. I use small and chunky seed beads in this book.

A small seed bead is one this size or smaller - o - sometimes called a size 10 or 12 and lower.

A chunky seed bead is one about this size - O - sometimes called a size 8.

Both small and chunky seeds come in different shapes and it does not matter for the designs in this book which you use. Just choose the colour and shape you like. Always test sew a few onto your fabric first.

Basic names for you to know are:
- ●   o   moulded rocaille
- ●   □   2/cut seed
- ●   ◻   3/cut seed

BUGLE BEADS
Bugle beads are long tubes of glass, plastic or metal and come in various lengths, from 2 mm to 4-5 cm long ($\frac{1}{16}$" to $1\frac{1}{2}$ - 2"). The designs in this book use:
- ●   size 1, 2-3 mm ($\frac{1}{16}$" - $\frac{1}{8}$") long
- ●   size 2, 5-6 mm ($\frac{1}{4}$") long
- ●   size 3, 10-12 mm ($\frac{3}{8}$") long

The size most commonly used is 2.

SEQUINS
Sequins are round pieces of metal or plastic with a hole in the centre, or to one side.

They can be either flat or cupped and come in various sizes. The designs in this book use 5 mm ($\frac{1}{8}$") and 6 mm ($\frac{1}{4}$") cup sequins, and 10 mm ($\frac{3}{8}$") flat sequins. The most common sequin available is the 6 mm cup sequin and may be used in all the designs if the 5 mm size is not available. Flat sequins with a hole to one side are used in the sequin flower on page 22.

Always check sequins carefully for colour fastness and washability as it is heartbreaking to find they fade the first time you wash them.

CENTRE BEADS
A centre bead is a larger bead used as a feature for the middle of a flower, the end of a dangle, or as an ending to a row of beads. There is a huge range available and quality varies greatly. Cheap plastic centres are not going to last long or look as beautiful as glass or metal.

The sizes I have used in this book are small, approximately 4-5 mm ($\frac{1}{8}$") (round or cut); large, approximately 6-7 mm ($\frac{1}{4}$") (round or oval cut); extra large oval stones are used on the jacket. They may have a hole through the centre or a hole on each side.

Rhinestones are usually made from glass with a metal back which has a cross on the back like this.

To sew these on, pass the thread through the cross and into the fabric in one direction, then repeat in the other direction to secure it flat onto your fabric. You may use rhinestones in place of a centre bead wherever you like.

OVAL OR RICE BEADS
Oval or rice beads are so called because of their shape – they are used as a spacer in dangles or as a feature beside a row of beading. They also make a nice flower when sewn on their own around a centre bead. Sew them on the same way as bugle beads. The most common size is about 1 cm ($\frac{1}{2}$") long.

DROPS
A drop bead can be any shaped or round bead which is larger than the other seed beads or bugle beads you use at the end of a dangle. Bi-cone beads are nice to use in the middle of a dangle or at the end. The dangles in this book use beads which have a hole through the centre of the bead, like this:

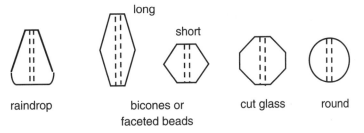

long   short

raindrop   bicones or faceted beads   cut glass   round

Drops which have a hole across the top are sewn on in a different way.

COLOURFAST CHECK

All your beads and sequins should be checked for colour fastness before you put them onto your garment or craft item. This is done by threading a few onto a piece of thread and placing them into a cup of warm water and mild washing liquid. Leave this to stand for a few minutes. If no colour is visible in the water, dip a white tissue into the water. The tissue will soak up the water and any small amount of colour will show up clearly. If no colour is present it is safe to use them. The beads which do lose colour may be used on items not likely to be washed, for example, the brooches, needle case or pin cushion in this book.

FABRICS

For the beginner I suggest a knit fabric – either a double knit, rugby or fleece. Most fabrics (woven and knit) are suitable. Extremely sheer fabrics, or ones which crush easily, are not recommended as pressing beaded work is difficult.

If you choose a fine fabric you may need to use an iron-on backing. I use Whisperweft® and Armoweft® from McCalls. Follow the manufacturer's instructions for use. If these are unavailable choose a good quality iron-on woven interfacing.

Here is a basic guide to fabrics which need to be backed or don't need to be backed:

NEED TO BE BACKED	interlock, fine rugby knits, some single knits, soft woven fabrics like crepe, some fine microfibres
DON'T NEED TO BE BACKED	double knit or faille. Some single knits are firm enough. Fleecy knits, woven poly/linen, heavy microfibres, raw silk, heavy crepe or wool crepe

NOTE: Remember to pre-wash your knits.

For the shawl design in this book you may use microfibre or crepe de chine, etc. Use a spray fabric stiffener to give you a firm fabric to bead. After it is washed, the stiffener will dissolve and you will be left with a very soft beaded fabric. This method is only suitable for some designs and extreme care is needed to keep the design flat on the fabric. The back of the work needs to be neat as it is visible.

NOTE: machine knits will need Whisperweft® behind them to stabilise the fabric for beading.

THREADS

Rasant thread or Mölnlycke are the threads least likely to twist. If you have a problem with the thread twisting, use a beeswax block and run the thread over this once, then wipe off the excess wax on a spare piece of fabric.

The thread should match the colour of the fabric, not the colour of the beads, although there are exceptions. For example, black beads on white fabric might look better using black thread. Do a test first to determine which looks best.

When sewing on sequins, the thread should match the sequin, not the fabric.

NEEDLES

Use good quality beading needles, sizes 10-13. Some brands have larger eyes than others. The biggest eyes are on the thicker needles (size 10 is the largest). The best needle threaders to use are the ones with red plastic ends, they are finer and go through the eye more easily.

CARING FOR YOUR BEADED GARMENT

WASHING: Use Lux® or Softly® and hand wash gently. Rinse well and wrap your garment in a towel. Gently squeeze out the excess water. Lay the garment flat to dry in the shade. Never tumble dry.

PRESSING: Do not press beading which has sequins on it as the heat from your iron will flatten your sequins. Beads may be pressed if you lay the work, right side facing down, over a towel and, with your iron on a wool setting, press gently from the back. If you are careful when you wash and dry your garment, laying it flat, you shouldn't need to press behind the beading. This is why fabric choice is important.

LEATHER: If you are using leather pieces for your appliqué, wash the pieces first in hair shampoo until all excess dye is removed. The beaded garment should always be washed in hair shampoo to keep the leather supple.

CHAPTER TWO

TRANSFERRING YOUR DESIGN

FIRST METHOD

Simply lay the fabric over the design and trace directly onto fabric, using either a blue water-soluble pen or coloured dressmaker's pencil. This only works if you can see the design through the fabric. Use a light box if you have one.

SECOND METHOD

For this you will need a piece of nylon organza (not crystal nylon organza) in a light colour, preferably white. You will need it a little larger than the design. Lay the organza over the design, pin in place. Trace the design onto the organza, using a permanent marker pen or a good quality pen. Allow this to dry completely before using. This tracing becomes your design template and can be used over and over again without damaging it.

Next, position this template onto your fabric and pin it in place. Trace over your template. For light colours use a blue water-soluble pen or coloured dressmaker's pencil. For dark colours use a white 'pastel' pencil or white dressmaker's pencil. If you are having trouble keeping the design visible on dark colours you can do one of two things. Either

- run a row of small tacking stitches around the design. The tacking is easily removed after beading.
  OR
- spray over the chalk-traced design with spray fabric stiffener to set the chalk to the fabric. This is sometimes enough to set the chalk while you are beading and is easily removed when washed.

NOTE: Always check first, whichever method you choose, that the ink can be removed from your fabric. Use clean water to remove blue ink as some washing powders can set the ink onto the fabric. Do not press over the blue ink as this also may cause it to set.

TRANSFER PENCILS

These are very useful for light colours, although some testing is needed to make sure the marking can be removed after beading, and also that the heat needed to set the design will not damage the fabric. I find the best pencil to use is an U.S.A. Birch™. It is a red pencil with a silver tip.

To use one of these you will need to trace the design onto greaseproof kitchen paper with the transfer pencil. Press firmly and sharpen the pencil regularly to keep your lines clear. Place the design onto your garment and pin in place. Lay a pressing cloth or brown paper over the top. Press with a warm iron on 'wool' setting. Do not move the iron back and forth but lift and press. Do not press over pins!

Now you are ready to begin beading.

PREPARING A TOP OR GARMENT FOR BEADING

Select your design and style of top. Choose the colour of beads and the type of fabric. Sometimes it is easier to choose your beads first as there is a larger colour choice in fabrics. If your fabric needs to be backed, only the area to be beaded needs to be covered. Cut the backing a bit larger than the design, taking it to the neckline edge or shoulder, etc., as this will support your beading.

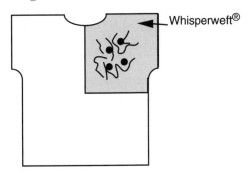

If you want your design to go over the shoulder, sew the shoulder seam together first. Also, if the beads are going to be very close to the neckline, it is a good idea to finish the neckline edge before you begin beading.

Trace the design onto the organza, as explained on page 6.

Position the design on the top, and check that you don't have the design in an inappropriate place, i.e. under your arm! Adjust where necessary. You can cut the design up or change part of it as you wish to suit the style of the top.

TRY IT ON

This method also allows you to get an idea of how the design will look when finished as it shows up well on all colours, even black!

Have a few design templates ready and try each one until you have the design which suits the garment and you best. When you are happy with the design placing, trace it using one of the methods for either dark or light colours described on page 6 .

Now you have your garment ready for beading!

CHAPTER THREE

HOW TO BEGIN

It is a good idea to practise before you actually begin beading your item. Use the same fabric and press a piece of Whisperweft® onto the back (this makes it easier for beginners to handle). Draw on a few lines to follow. Tip a few beads onto a spare piece of fabric on a tray (this stops the beads running away). It is easy to make a bead tray by gluing a piece of fabric onto a plastic plate – very portable. Thread your needle with a double thickness of thread (not too long or you will end up in a tangle). Knot the end.

Bring the thread through from the back of the fabric at the beginning of a line. Take a small whip stitch or backstitch to secure the thread. This must be done at the beginning of all beading and is called a support stitch.

Work towards you unless the pattern requires you to have the beads on the opposite angle, in which case you work away from yourself. Keep your line at right angles to you at all times – this is important when beading around a curve to get the beads on the same angle all the way around.

The space between the beads should be big enough to pass the beading needle through easily. The beads should not touch.

The thread passes through the beads on an angle, but the stitch at the back of the fabric is straight across.

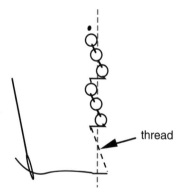

thread

Left-handed students will need to work from left to right.

IMPORTANT
Always remember that where the thread comes through the fabric is where the next bead will lie. Make sure it is positioned accurately, especially when turning corners, e.g. for the arms of a flower.

CHAPTER FOUR

BEADING STITCHES

1. Seed beads one at a time
2. Seed beads three at a time
3. Bugle beads with a whip stitch
4   Bugle bead and seed bead
5. Three seed beads, one sequin
6. Three seed beads, one sequin, one bead, one sequin
7. Bugle beads one at a time
8. Bugle beads with loops across
9. Sequins one at a time
10. Raised chain stitch
11. Feather stitch
12. Bugle bead with back stitch
13. Centre bead with seeds around
14. Centre bead with loops around
15. Cluster centre
16. Twisted leaf

FLOWERS

17. Central large flower
18. Split leaf flower
19. Spider flower
20. Flat sequin flower
21. Finger flower

22. Basic dangles
23. Split dangles
24. Sequin spotting
25. Seed bead spotting
26. Edges

1. SEED BEADS ONE AT A TIME

● Support stitch, continue: thread a single seed bead onto the needle. Hold it in place on the line and make a stitch at the bottom of the bead, the same size as the bead, across the fabric from right to left.

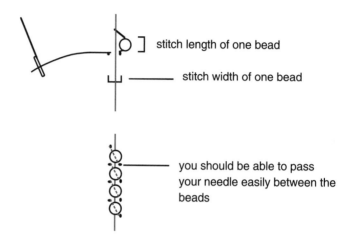

stitch length of one bead

stitch width of one bead

you should be able to pass your needle easily between the beads

2. SEED BEADS THREE AT A TIME

● Support stitch, continue: thread three seed beads onto the needle. Hold them in place on the line. Sew them on using a whip stitch across the fabric from right to left, below the last bead.

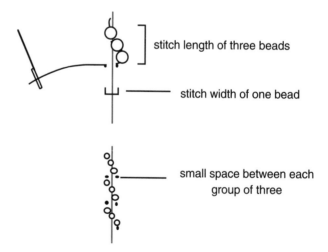

stitch length of three beads

stitch width of one bead

small space between each group of three

NOTE: the beads will be on a slight angle.

3. BUGLE BEADS WITH A WHIP STITCH

● Support stitch, continue: thread one bugle bead onto the needle and take a whip stitch, working from right to left across the fabric, the length of the bugle bead. The stitch you take should be the **width** of the bead.

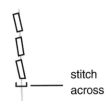

stitch across

NOTE: the beads will sit at a slight angle.

4. BUGLE BEAD AND SEED BEAD

● Support stitch, continue: thread one bugle bead onto the needle and sew on using a whip stitch working from right to left across the fabric, the length of the bugle bead.

● Then thread a seed bead onto the needle and sew on using a whip stitch, working from right to left across the fabric, the length of the seed bead.

● Continue alternating one bugle, one seed bead, along the line.

Beads should be on a slight angle and slightly spaced apart.

5. THREE SEED BEADS, ONE SEQUIN

● Support stitch, continue: thread three seed beads and one sequin onto your needle in this way:

● Take a whip stitch, working from right to left across the fabric, the length of the three seed beads along the pattern line. Beads should be on an angle with the sequin sitting curved side down, flat on the fabric.

NOTE: the sequin is picked up by putting the point of the needle into the cup of the sequin.

6. THREE SEED BEADS, ONE SEQUIN, ONE BEAD, ONE SEQUIN

● Thread three seed beads, one sequin, one bead, one sequin onto your needle in this way:

Sew onto your fabric in the same manner as the previous stitch.

7. BUGLE BEADS ONE AT A TIME

● Support stitch, continue: bring the thread up through the fabric at point A end of the placement line, thread on one bugle bead and put needle back in at point B and up through the fabric at point A again.

● Put the needle back in at A and come up at the beginning of the placement line for the next bugle bead. As long as the placement lines for your bugle beads are not more than 1.5 cm ($\frac{5}{8}$") apart, there is no need to cut the thread in between.

8. BUGLE BEADS WITH LOOPS ACROSS

● Support stitch, continue: thread one bugle bead onto the needle. Take a whip stitch, working from right to left across the fabric, the length of the bead. Leave a space the size of one seed bead before whip stitching the next bugle bead on (it may help if you put a small whip stitch in between).

- When you have completed your row in this manner, end off your work and go back to the beginning.

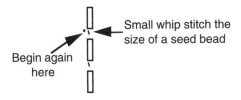

Begin again here

Small whip stitch the size of a seed bead

- Bring the needle up where shown in the diagram above and take a small support stitch. Thread five or six small seed beads onto the needle and loop them across the space between the bugle beads.

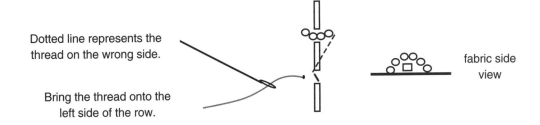

Dotted line represents the thread on the wrong side.

Bring the thread onto the left side of the row.

fabric side view

9. SEQUINS ONE AT A TIME

- Support stitch, continue: thread a sequin onto the needle by putting the point of the needle into the cup.

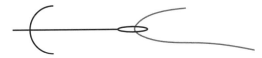

- Take a tiny whip stitch, the same width from the hole in the sequin to the outside edge, away from the starting point.

Take a tiny stitch

L ← R

This distance

● The next sequin is sewn on by taking another tiny whip stitch, right to left underneath the outside edge of the previous sequin.

● The stitch should not be seen. The hole in the sequins should be covered slightly by the edge of the one in front. No thread should be visible on the following sequins. Use thread to match the sequin colour, not the fabric.

10. RAISED CHAIN STITCH

● Support stitch, continue: thread eight beads (chunky or small) onto the needle. Put the needle into the fabric, on the line, the length of seven beads (point A). Bring the needle back up 5 or 6 mm (¼") along the line, to the right of the row of beads.

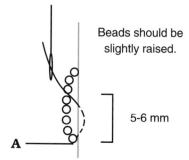

Beads should be slightly raised.

5-6 mm

A

● Thread eight beads onto the needle. Put the needle into the fabric at point B and come back up at point A, to the right of the row of beads (see diagram).

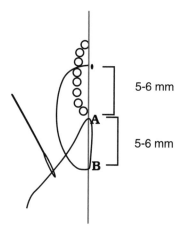

5-6 mm

A

5-6 mm

B

The beads will form interlocking loops.

- Repeat this, always coming back up on the same side and taking your stitches exactly on the line drawn on your fabric.

This stitch is a back stitch.

11. FEATHER STITCH

- Support stitch, continue: sew a row of seed beads, three or four at a time, towards you. To the left of this row, sew away from yourself, three or four seed beads at a time.

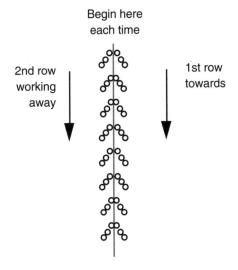

Begin here
each time

2nd row
working
away

1st row
towards

- The second row will match up with the first row to form 'V' shapes with the sets of three beads. Always begin at the point of the 'V' (see diagram).

12. BUGLE BEAD WITH BACK STITCH

- Support stitch, continue: for this stitch you must remember to start your stitches the length of one bugle bead from the beginning.

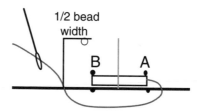

- Thread one bugle bead onto the needle. Lay this bead along the line and put the needle in at the beginning point A. Bring the needle out on the line, half the length of a bugle bead from point B.

- The next bugle bead lies to the right-hand side of the first bead.

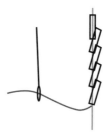

- Put the needle in halfway along the first bead and bring the needle out half a bugle bead length away from the bead's end. Continue in this way, keeping the beads on the same angle. This forms a stem stitch in beads.

13. CENTRE BEAD WITH SEEDS AROUND

- Support stitch, continue: sew the central bead in place, taking a stitch the same size as the bead and

sewing it on twice to secure. Bring the thread up beside
the central bead at point A. Thread four or five small
seed beads onto the needle and lay them around the
bead (they should only go halfway around) to point B.
Take a stitch in at the last bead and come up on the
other side of the central bead at starting point A.

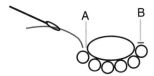

- Thread enough small seed beads onto the needle to
  wrap around to the other side. The beads should fit
  neatly around the central bead.

14. CENTRE BEAD WITH LOOPS AROUND

- Support stitch, continue: sew the central bead in place,
  taking a stitch the same size as the bead and sewing it
  on twice to secure. Bring the thread up beside the
  central bead at point A. Divide the bead into three
  sections (using a water soluble pen if you need to mark
  points).

- Thread seven small seed beads onto the needle and put
  the needle in at point B. Come up at point C. Thread
  another seven small beads onto the needle and put the
  needle in at point B, coming up at point A.

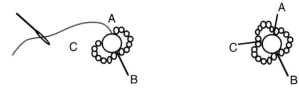

- Thread another seven small seed beads onto the
  needle and put the needle in at point C. This will form
  the last loop. Depending on how many small seeds you
  use, you can make the loops large or small. For larger
  centre beads do four loops of beads around.

15. CLUSTER CENTRE

- Support stitch, continue: thread a large seed bead onto the needle, then a small bead. Hold the small bead and take the thread back through the large bead and down through the fabric.

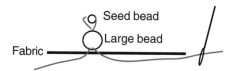

- Stitch these around in a cluster. Some can have two small seeds on top.

OR

- Thread a bugle bead and seed bead onto the needle, hold the seed bead and thread the needle back through the bugle bead only, then into the fabric.

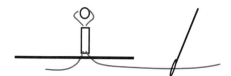

DOUBLE BUGLE BEAD CLUSTER

Support stitch, continue: thread one bugle bead, one seed bead, then one bugle bead onto the needle. Take the thread back down into the fabric, the width of the seed bead away from the starting point.

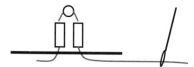

TIP: Pull the thread firmly on all your cluster beads as they look too floppy if left loose.

16. TWISTED LEAF

Support stitch, continue: thread eight small seed beads onto your needle. Lay them on the fabric where the leaf is to go. Take a tiny stitch at the end of the last bead and bring the needle up one bead back from the end.

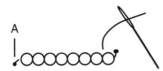

- Thread another eight beads onto the needle and cross them over the first row (see solid line denoting the second row of beads in the diagram below).

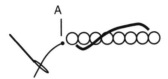

- Put the needle into the fabric one bead back from point A. Secure at the back. This stitch may be done with any number of small seeds to give various-sized leaves.

17. CENTRAL LARGE FLOWER

- Draw the guide shown below, making the centre circle the size of the central bead you are using. Make sure that the radiating lines are straight and at right angles to the central bead.

- Support stitch, continue: sew on a central bead, taking a stitch the same size as the bead. Sew through the bead twice to secure.

- Thread should come up beside the central bead at the base of one of the side lines. Thread three beads, one sequin, one bead, one sequin, one bead and one sequin onto the needle. Take a stitch out from the central bead so that the beads are arched and the last sequin is flat onto the fabric.

  NOTE: the sequins are picked up by putting the point of the needle into the cup of the sequin.

- Bring the needle up beside the central bead at the base of the line on the opposite side (see diagram below). Take a small support stitch beside the central bead.

- Work each of the four sides of the flower this way. On the last side, bring the needle up in between two sections beside the central bead. The next four sections are then done as follows – thread three beads, one sequin, one bead, one sequin only onto the needle. Take a stitch (not quite as long as for the first four sections) out from the central bead in between two sides. Take a support stitch after each row as before.

TIP: keep the sides at right angles to the central bead. Position your thread accurately.

18. SPLIT LEAF FLOWER

- Support stitch, continue: sew a central bead onto the fabric. Take a stitch the same size as the bead and sew through twice to secure.

SPLIT LEAF
- Thread seven small seed beads onto the needle. Lay them on the fabric where the leaf is to go. Take a tiny stitch at the end of the last bead. Put the needle back

into the fabric at the end of the last bead and bring it up at the starting point.

TIP: this flower looks best done in small beads – you can adjust the number of beads to make smaller or larger petals.

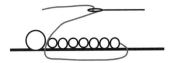

● Thread the same amount of beads onto the needle and lay these beads alongside the first row.

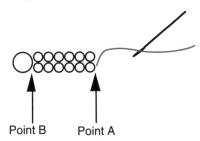

Point B   Point A

● Put needle back down into the fabric in the same place as previous row (point A). Bring it up between the two rows, two beads from point A.

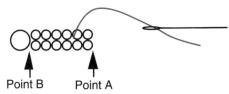

Point B   Point A

● Thread five or six small seed beads onto the needle and take a stitch two or three bead widths from point A.

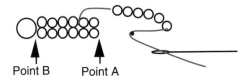

Point B   Point A

● These beads will split the two rows to form the flowers. They should be slightly raised.

Top view   Side view

● Repeat as many times as needed for your flower (i.e. five petals, six petals, etc).

19. SPIDER FLOWER

● Support stitch, continue: Sew the central bead with a whip stitch the same size as the bead. Sew through twice to secure. Bring the needle up through the fabric at the beginning of one of the rows near the central bead. Thread any number of beads you need onto the needle and stitch the length of the line. Take a small support stitch. See the first step of the split leaf flower. Bring the needle up at the beginning of the next line and do the same thing. Work all around the central bead in this way.

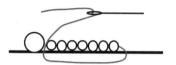

20. FLAT SEQUIN FLOWER

● For this flower you will need sequins which look like this, with a hole to one side.

● Begin by sewing on a large central bead, either a 1 cm (³⁄₈") pearl or an oval dress stone. The pearl may be sewn on in the same manner as a bead cluster, i.e. by using a small seed to anchor over the hole. Make sure you end this off securely.

● Do four loops of nine or ten beads around it, you may use chunky beads or small beads.

● Bring the thread up close to the pearl. Thread onto your needle one flat sequin, one chunky bead, one flat sequin, one chunky bead, one flat sequin.

- Take a stitch out from the pearl, approximately 1 cm (⅜") long, bring the needle up on the opposite side of the pearl.

NB: Loops not shown

The last sequin will sit flat on the fabric.

- Continue working around the pearl until you have filled your flower in, or until you have covered all spaces. The size of the finished flower depends on which size seed beads you use.

21. FINGER FLOWER

The basic rule to remember before you begin this flower is that each row of beads must form a loop approximately the same size. Beads which are irregular in size will make this difficult. For the Lily petals, follow the pattern for placement of loops. To make a five-petal flower, work as follows (adjust the number of beads according to the size you are using).

- Sew on a 1 cm (⅜") dress stone and secure at the back. Bring the needle up close to the dress stone in the middle of a petal.

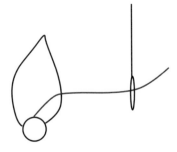

- Thread up eight beads. Lay them onto the fabric and put the needle into the fabric level with the seventh bead.

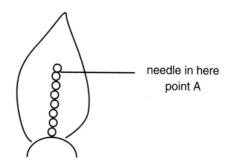

needle in here
point A

● Bring the needle up close to the dress stone and beside the first row of beads.

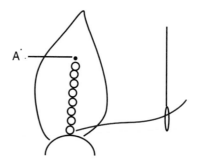

A

● Thread up eight beads and put the needle into the fabric one bead back from point A. Bring the needle up close to the dress stone on the other side and thread up another eight beads – repeat the loop on this side.

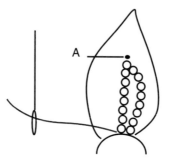

A

● Bring the needle up close to, and above, point A.

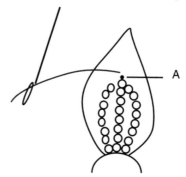

A

● Thread up eight beads and repeat as for first row of beads, laying the beads along to the point of the petal at point B.

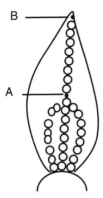

● Bring the needle up one bead back from point A.

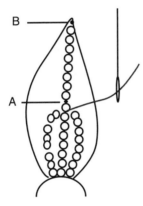

● Thread up eight beads and put the needle back into the fabric two beads back from point B. Bring the needle up on the other side near point A and repeat the procedure for this side.

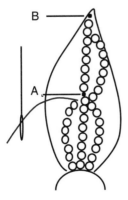

● Bring the needle up in between one of the first two loops and thread up eight beads. This time you need to tuck the needle slightly under the beads at point C.

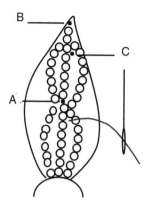

- Bring the needle up on the other side, in between the two lower loops, and repeat the procedure for that side.

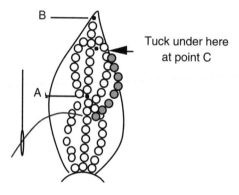

Tuck under here
at point C

- Eight rows of looped beads form one petal. Repeat for the other five petals.

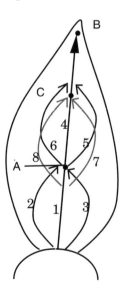

- When you have completed all the petals, fill in the spaces between with three or four beads and one sequin. It is easier to thread the sequin on through the dome side first, then thread the three or four seeds

and work out from the dress stone. Use four groups if
you have 5 mm sequins or one group for 6 mm sequins.

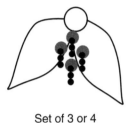

Set of 3 or 4

One

22. BASIC DANGLES

For this dangle use a bead with a hole through the length
of the bead, not across the top.

- Support stitch, continue: take an extra support stitch
  for dangles. Then thread any combination of beads
  onto the needle like this.

- When you have the correct length of beads, thread the
  large seed or drop onto the needle and one more seed
  bead, like this.

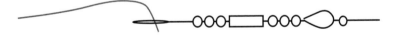

- Hold the last seed bead and thread the needle back
  down through the drop and other beads.

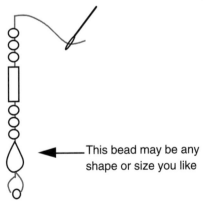

This bead may be any
shape or size you like

- Don't pull the thread too tight. Take another stitch at
  the top and then thread up another two or three
  dangles in different lengths.

23. SPLIT DANGLES

- Use a drop bead with a hole across the top, like this.

- Support stitch, continue: thread three or four seed beads onto the needle, then a large seed bead (or bi-cone bead), three or four small seed beads, the split drop and three or four small beads, like this.

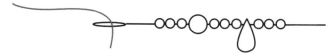

- Hold the four small seed beads, the drop, and the other four small seed beads and thread the needle back into the large bead and the first few seed beads.

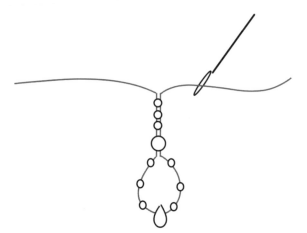

- Don't pull the thread too tight. Take another support stitch at the top and then thread up another two or three dangles in different lengths.

24. SEQUIN SPOTTING

- Support stitch, continue: the sequins need to be cup side up with a seed bead in the centre.

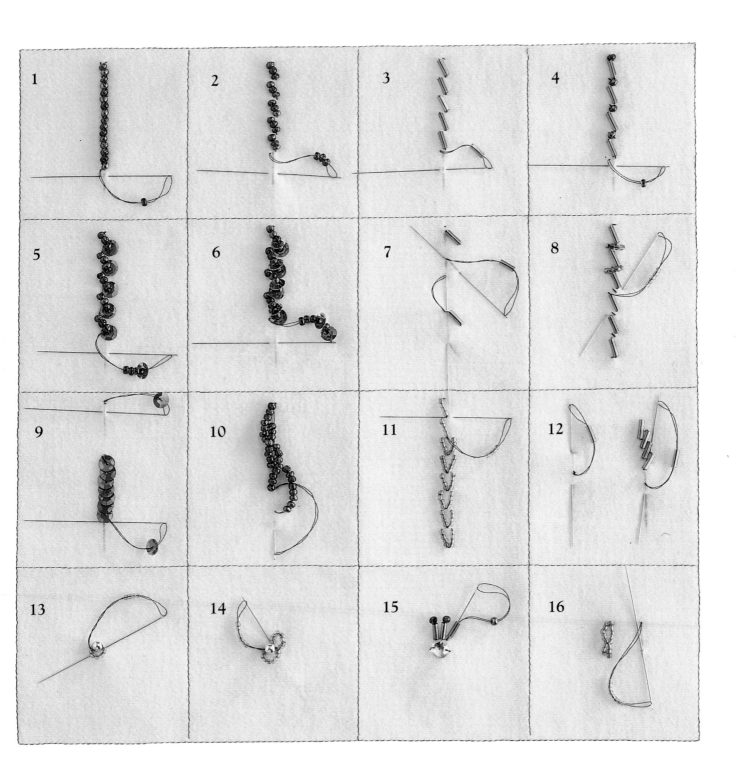

BEADING STITCHES

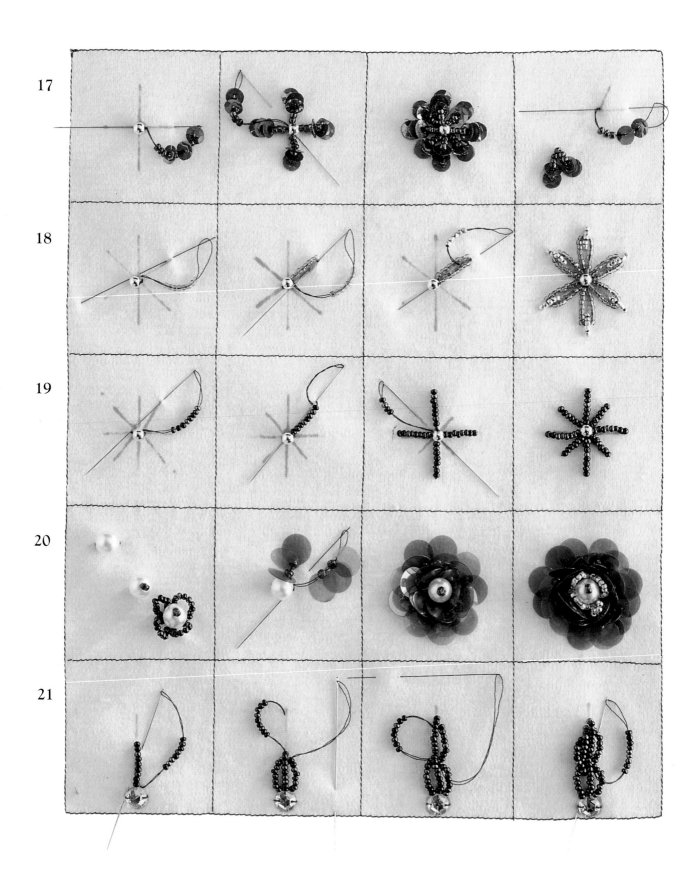

17

18

19

20

21

BEADING STITCHES

LONG-SLEEVED TOP

DETAIL, SHORT-SLEEVED TOP

DETAIL, LONG-SLEEVED TOP.

NECKLACE TOP

BROOCH

● This is done by picking up the sequin and threading onto the needle dome side first. Then thread on a seed bead. Hold the seed bead on the thread above the sequin and sew back down into the sequin. Pull through using the seed bead to hold the sequin onto the fabric. Follow the design for exact placement.

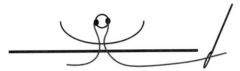

25. SEED BEAD SPOTTING

● Support stitch, continue: thread one seed bead onto the needle and whip stitch it in place. End off.

● Three in a triangle are sewn on one at a time. Spotting around a design blends the beading and enlarges the design. Try some!

26. EDGES

● Support stitch, continue: thread seven or eight small seed beads onto the needle. Take a stitch approximately 1 cm (³⁄₈") along the edge away from the starting point.

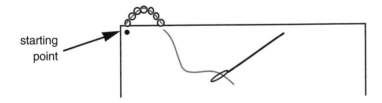

● If the fabric is thick, the needle should go into the very edge; if the fabric is thin the needle should go into the back and come out as on the diagram below.

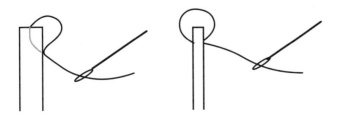

There are many other combinations of beads and bugle beads that can go around edges – here are two examples:

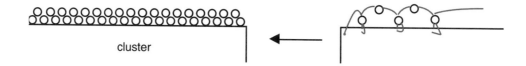

cluster

● *Cluster* – sew one bead onto your fabric using a whip stitch. Pass the thread back up through this bead. Now thread onto your needle two more beads and stitch them on one bead width away. Pass the needle back up through the last bead only and continue, adding two beads and passing the thread back through one. This is a form of needleweaving.

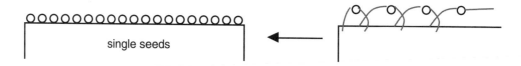

single seeds

● *Single seed edge* – sew one bead onto the edge as shown in the diagram above. Loop the thread back around the bead and then sew on another bead. By looping the thread around each time, you straighten the bead and make it secure.

TURNING CORNERS

● For turning corners using single seed beads, or three seed beads at a time, take a small stitch at the end of the last bead and bring the needle up one or two beads back along the line.

tiny stitch

● Turn the work and then continue down the other side, leaving one or two beads for the point of the leaf.

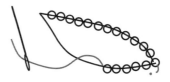

CHAPTER FIVE

PROJECTS AND DESIGNS

LONG-SLEEVED PALE GREEN TOP

You may either make your own, or put this design on a ready-made top.

REQUIREMENTS

3 x 5 g (¼ oz) packets small seed beads in main colour
2 x 5 g (¼ oz) packets small seed beads in contrast colour
1 x 5 g (¼ oz) packet bugle beads
18 x size 5 mm (¼") cut beads or 5 mm (¼") centre beads

PREPARATION FOR BEADING

- Join only the left shoulder seam of your top.
- Follow the instructions on page 6 for transferring your design and applying backing if required.

BEADING INSTRUCTIONS

Begin beading, working from the back panel of your top to the front.
- Row 1: bugle beads with loops across (do the loops in contrast colour).
- Row 2: raised chain stitch in main colour seeds.
- Row 3: feather stitch, one side main colour, one side contrast colour.
  Then sew your cut beads or centres in position at the end of each row.

TIP: adjust the number of beads to fit neatly over the crossing points.

TO FINISH YOUR TOP

- Rinse out all traces of blue pen or chalk. Allow to dry.
- Complete the garment as your pattern indicates.

There are many variations to this design. Experiment and see what other combinations you can come up with.

LONG SLEEVED TOP

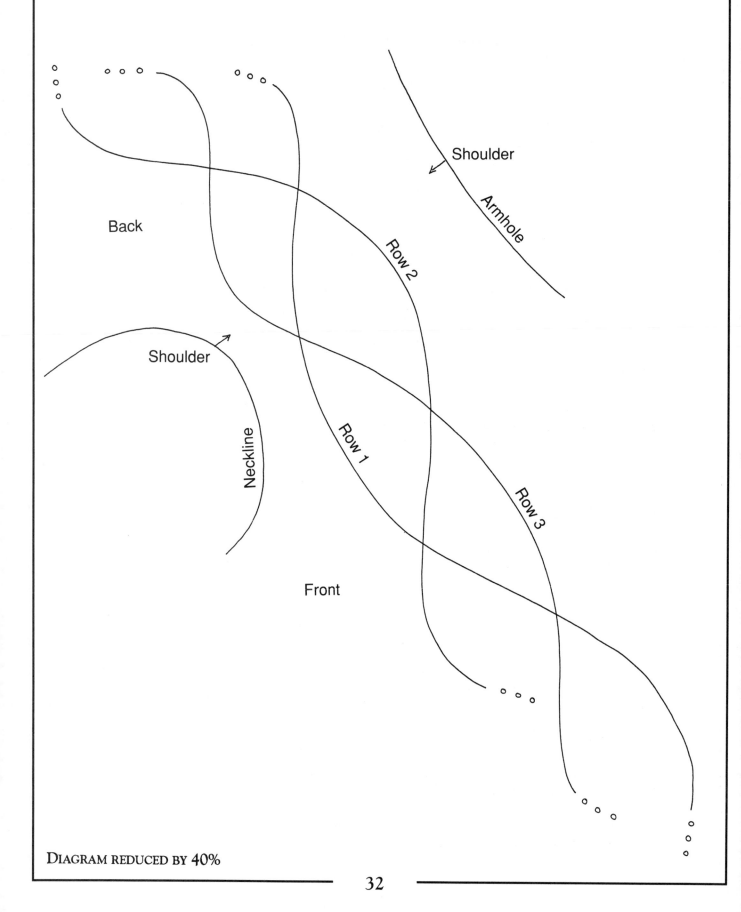

Shoulder

Armhole

Back

Row 2

Shoulder

Neckline

Row 1

Front

Row 3

SHORT-SLEEVED TOP

You may either make your own, or put this design on a ready-made top.

REQUIREMENTS

STEMS AND LEAVES	2 x 5 g (¼ oz) packets small seeds
SPIDER FLOWER	1x 5 g (¼ oz) packets small seeds
SPLIT LEAF FLOWER	1 x 5 g (¼ oz) packets small seeds
SEQUIN FLOWER	1 x 3 g (⅛ oz) packets sequins
	8 x 5 mm (¼") centre beads

PREPARATION FOR BEADING

- Join together both shoulder seams of your top.
- Finish the neckline edge.
- Follow the instructions on page 6 for transferring design and applying backing if required.

BEADING INSTRUCTIONS

- Split leaf flower and single petals.
- Central large flower.
- Spider flower and radiating lines.

TIP: Don't carry the threads more than 1.5 cm (⅝") across the back of your work.

- Now join the flowers together by doing the stems, three seed beads at a time.
- Leaves may be either a single split leaf or a twisted leaf
- Finish with seed spotting where indicated.

TO FINISH YOUR TOP

- Rinse out all traces of blue pen or chalk. Allow to dry.
- Complete the garment as your pattern indicates.

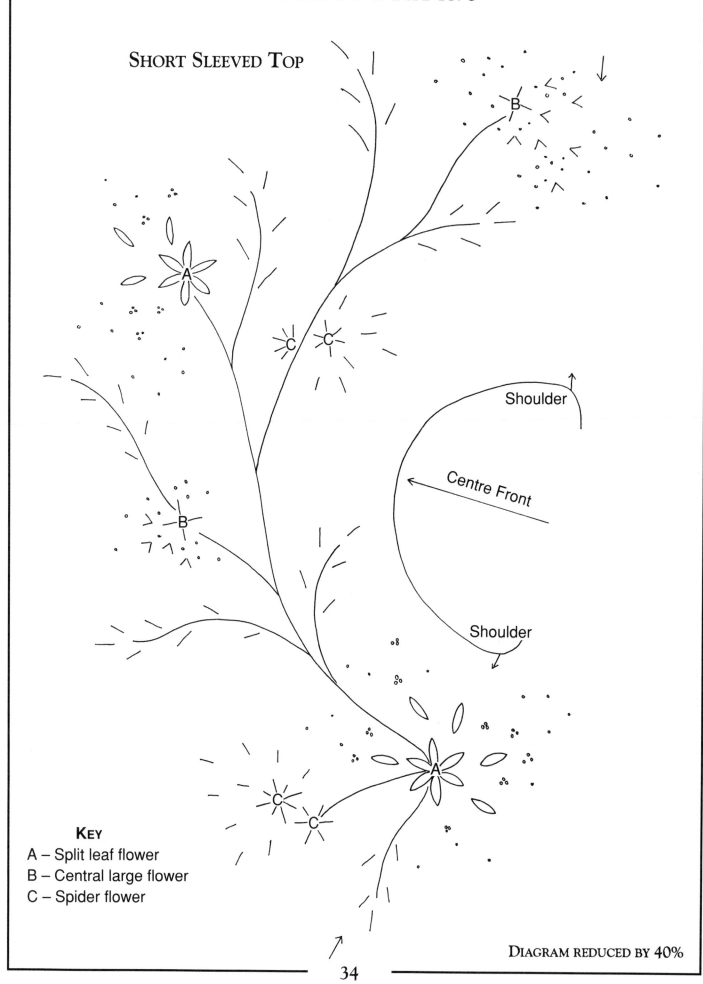

SHORT SLEEVED TOP

B

A

C C

Shoulder

Centre Front

Shoulder

B

A

C

C

KEY
A – Split leaf flower
B – Central large flower
C – Spider flower

DIAGRAM REDUCED BY 40%

PLUM NECKLACE TOP

This top has a detachable brooch/pendant. Two styles are given.

REQUIREMENTS

1 ready-made fine knit jumper with a high crew neckline.
1 brooch back (no longer than 2 cm [¾"])
5 cm x 12 cm (2" x 4¾") of fabric the same colour as your jumper
5 cm x 12 cm (2" x 4¾") iron-on Vilene
5 cm x 6 cm (2" x 2½")piece of Vliesafix

BEADS

3 x 5 g (¼ oz) packets seed beads, may be different colours
6 x 7 mm (¼") dress stones
1 x 3 g (⅛ oz) sequins
1 x 1.2 cm (½") oval dress stone
3 drop beads for pendant No 2
3 bi-cone beads for pendant No 2

PREPARING YOUR JUMPER FOR BEADING

● Roll the neckline band in half. Pin and tack in place on the seamline.

1. Right side

2. Right side. Roll over

3. Right side. Stitch in place on the seamline

● Slip stitch the edge in place on the seamline.
Your banding is now rolled over and is half the width.

BEADING INSTRUCTIONS FOR THE NECK EDGE

- Loops of beads are sewn over the rolled neckline. Begin at the shoulder on the inside of the neckline.
- Thread enough seeds onto the needle to go over the rolled band on a slight angle. My loops are 3 cm (1¼") apart. Measure the neckline edge first to make sure you will have loops evenly spaced all the way around.
- Remember, you will need to stretch the neckline a bit to get it over your head – so don't put the loops any further apart than 3 cm (1¼").
- Mark the centre of your jumper front and tack. Mark with pins where you want the necklace to sit and also tack along this line.
- Mark where the 'pendant' will go in the centre. Tack around this line as well.
- TRY IT ON and adjust if necessary.

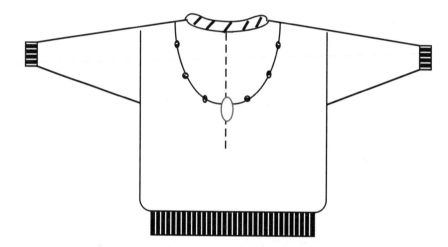

BEADING INSTRUCTIONS FOR THE CHAIN

- Divide each side into four equal sections from the centre to the shoulder seam.
- Sew a round dress stone at the points dividing these sections.
- NB: There is no dress stone at the shoulder seam.
- Follow your tacking thread and join the dress stones from the shoulder to the centre on both sides.

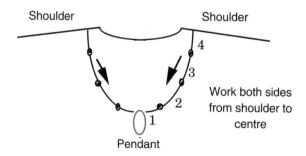

● The stitch I have used is raised chain stitch. You may alternate the colours as you go. Try to join the rows neatly in the centre. Remove the tacking thread beneath these rows.

PREPARATION OF THE PENDANT BACKING

● Press the Vilene onto the wrong side of fabric.
● Press the Vliesafix onto one half of the Vilene. Peel away the paper. Fold the fabric in half and press. This gives you a very firm working medium which will not fray easily.
● Mark the oval shape onto this thick fabric.

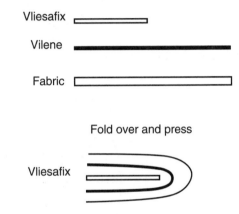

Vliesafix

Vilene

Fabric

Fold over and press

Vliesafix

● Using a small straight stitch, sew around the marked oval shape.

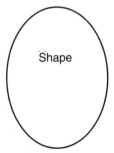

Shape

● Cut out the shape close to stitching.

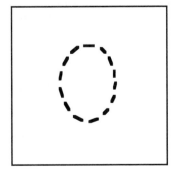

● Using a small zigzag stitch, sew over the edge again.

Allow the machine to make one stitch off the fabric and one on, this overcasts the edge.

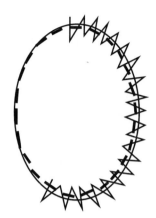

- Mark the centre, quarters and eighths on the oval shape.

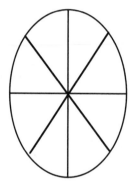

BEADING INSTRUCTIONS

PENDANT NO 1

- Work a raised chain stitch around the edge using six beads for each loop instead of eight.
- Sew the oval dress stone in place.
- Around this stone do four loops of eight small seed beads. Then do another row of four loops of 10 small seed beads. The second row will be alternate spacing.

First row —————

Second row —————

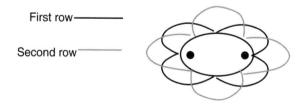

This gives you a rose effect in the centre.

● At each of the divisions marked do one central large flower petal.

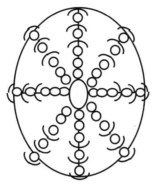

● I have used my second colour seeds to do another group of petals in between. You may use a contrast bead and sequin instead.

PENDANT NO 2

● Around the edge of this fabric I have beaded a cluster edge. The only change I have made is to add one seed bead onto the needle before passing the needle up through the last bead.

This edging forms the 'frame'. It is easier to do this with moulded beads as they sit better than cut beads.

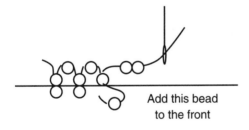

Add this bead
to the front

● Sew the oval dress stone in position and do two rows of loops, the same as for Pendant No 1.
● At the positions marked, work a central large flower petal in the main colour.

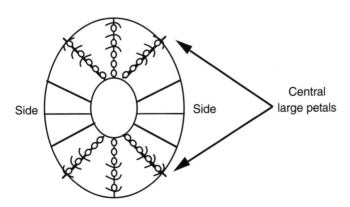

Side   Side   Central
large petals

- At the side positions sew three loops of beads. The number of beads used will vary depending on the size you are using.
- In the spaces left, sew a central large flower petal in a contrast colour.

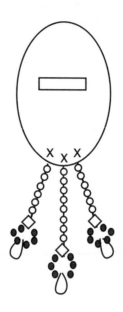

- Split dangles are sewn onto the pendant at the back of the lower edge.

TO FINISH BOTH PENDANTS

- Sew a brooch back securely onto the back of each pendant.

GOLD BROOCH

REQUIREMENTS

Gold brooch surround – must be at least 3.5 cm long and 3.5 cm wide (1¼" x 1¼")
3 g (⅛ oz) flat gold sequins with a hole to one side
1.2 cm (½")oval dress stone
10 cut centres
1 x 5 g (¼ oz) packet small gold or bronze beads
Small piece of felt in a colour to blend with your beads
Gold thread
Glue

PREPARING THE BASE

- Cut out two ovals of felt to fit inside the brooch surround. Slip stitch these together.
- Mark the centre, then the quarter points and diagonal lines.

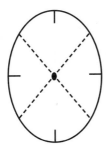

- Sew your centre oval bead in position. You may use the same method as for a cluster, and anchor the stone on with a small bead over the hole. This actually looks much better than a stitch on these larger stones.
- Now sew four loops of nine or 10 small seed beads around this oval. See instructions on page 17.
- Sew a split leaf petal at each diagonal line. You may need to reduce the number of beads to fit the petal in, working right to the edge of the felt.
- In between these split leaf petals, sew flat sequin petals. You should fit two in each space. Make sure that the last sequin sits over the edge of the felt.
- In the spaces left, sew dangles of various lengths. I have used seed beads and a centre bead only but if you like, use a few bugle beads or rice beads as well.
- If you can see felt behind some spots just fill in with single beads.
- Glue this flower to the middle of the brooch and leave to dry.

This flower on felt could also just have a plain brooch back stitched onto it and be used the same way as the pendant on the Necklace Top on page 35.

TEARDROP SCARF

REQUIREMENTS

70 cm x 115 cm (27½" x 45") of fabric (microfibre or crepe de chine are best)
Spray fabric stiffener – 'Helmar Sew Stable'® or three to four coats of Crisp® or Fabulon®
Thread to match your fabric

BEADS

1 oval 1.2 cm (½") dress stone
11 drops of your choice
21 oval rice beads
1 x 5 g (¼ oz) packet small seed beads
1 x 5 g (¼ oz) packet size 2 bugle beads
A few size 1 bugle beads (optional)
A few chunky seed beads for spotting

PREPARING YOUR SCARF

- Enlarge the pattern as instructed.
- Cut one piece of fabric, making sure you have it exactly on grain.
- Finish all the edges of the scarf. You may roll the hem using an overlocker, sewing machine, or by hand.

TIP: An easy way to do this is to stay stitch 6 mm (¼") in from the edge by machine. Fold this edge over on the stitching line and press. Trim the 6 mm (¼") back to 3 mm (⅛") and fold this edge over again.
    This will give you a neat 3 mm (⅛") hem.

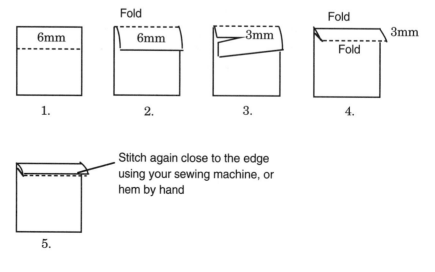

- Spray the area to be beaded with fabric stiffener (Helmar® brand is best). Allow to dry completely before proceeding.
- Mark the design onto the scarf using one of the methods described on page 6.

BEADING INSTRUCTIONS

- Begin beading by attaching the oval dress stone to the corner in the same way as explained for the Oriental pouch Bag. Make sure it is close to the edge.
- Begin sewing on the bugle beads with a back stitch, working from the oval bead. When going around the corners, slightly angle the beads. This takes a bit of practice but is worth the effort as the effect is beautiful. I also call this 'stem stitch in beads'.
- Next sew the bugle bead, seed bead line, working from the oval bead first. Then add in the last row, beginning from the centre of the design out to the top edge.
- The oval rice beads are sewn in place using the same method as for bugle beads – one at a time.
- The centre beads are sewn in next, where marked.
- Add seed spotting in the areas marked.

DANGLE ON THE BEADED CORNER

- The middle dangle is done first, then two on each side of it. Take a small support stitch at the back of the corner point, close to the hem. Form the dangles as follows.
- Work five dangles as shown. Each one has the same beads but is positioned higher up around the corner, as shown in the diagram below.

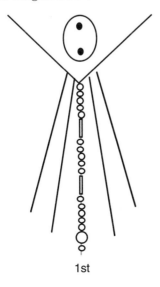

1st

DANGLES ON THE NARROW ENDS

- Sew an oval rice bead in place of the dress stone and work only three dangles, using the same beads as in the diagram above.

TO FINISH YOUR SCARF

- Rinse the scarf in clean warm water (no detergent) to remove all traces of stiffener and marking pen. Lay flat to dry.
- Form the pleats as marked and press them gently. You may catch the pleats down with a few tiny stitches on the wrong side. To wear the scarf, simply drape it with the longest end going around your neck and hanging down at the front. The shorter end goes over the top of this and hangs down the back. The design should drape to one side and slightly over your shoulder as shown in the picture. This scarf also looks beautiful with the Gold Brooch used to hold the scarf in place at the shoulder.

TEARDROP SCARF

GLASSES CASE &
BOOK COVER

FISH BOXES

DETAIL, EVENING JACKET

EVENING JACKET

NEEDLE CASE &
PIN CUSHION

GOLD BROOCH

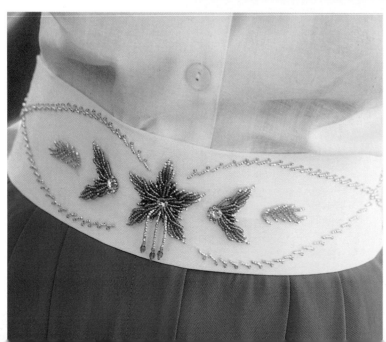

FLOWER BELT

GOLD TEARDROP SCARF

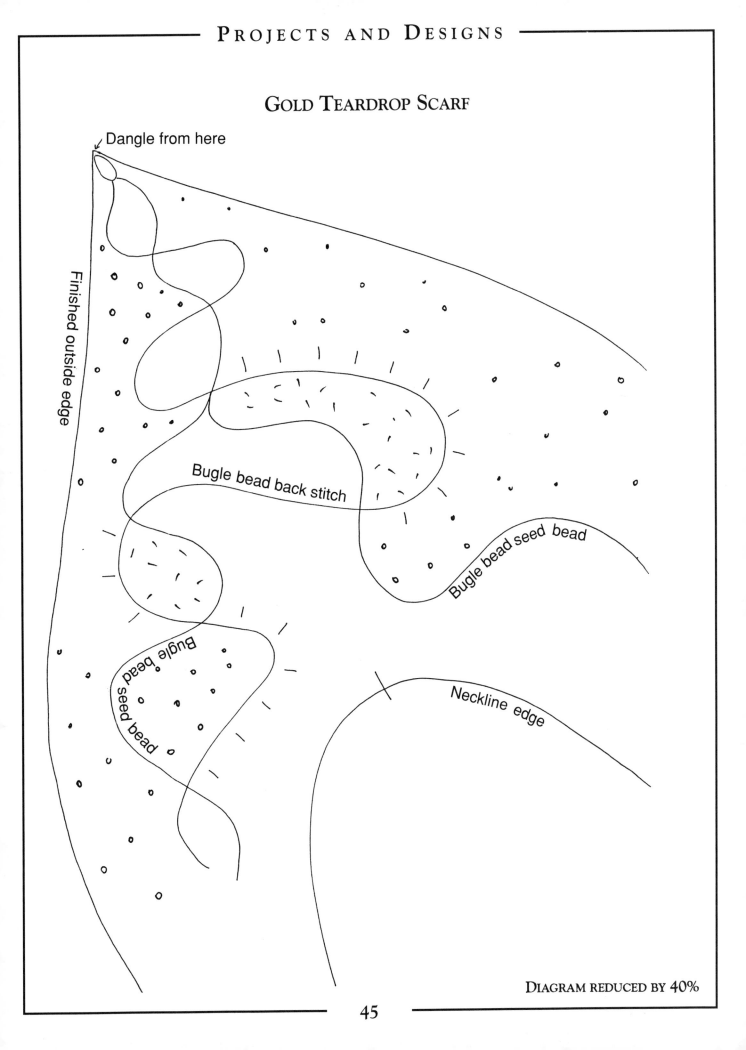

Dangle from here

Finished outside edge

Bugle bead back stitch

Bugle bead seed bead

Bugle bead seed bead

Neckline edge

DIAGRAM REDUCED BY 40%

GOLD TEARDROP SCARF

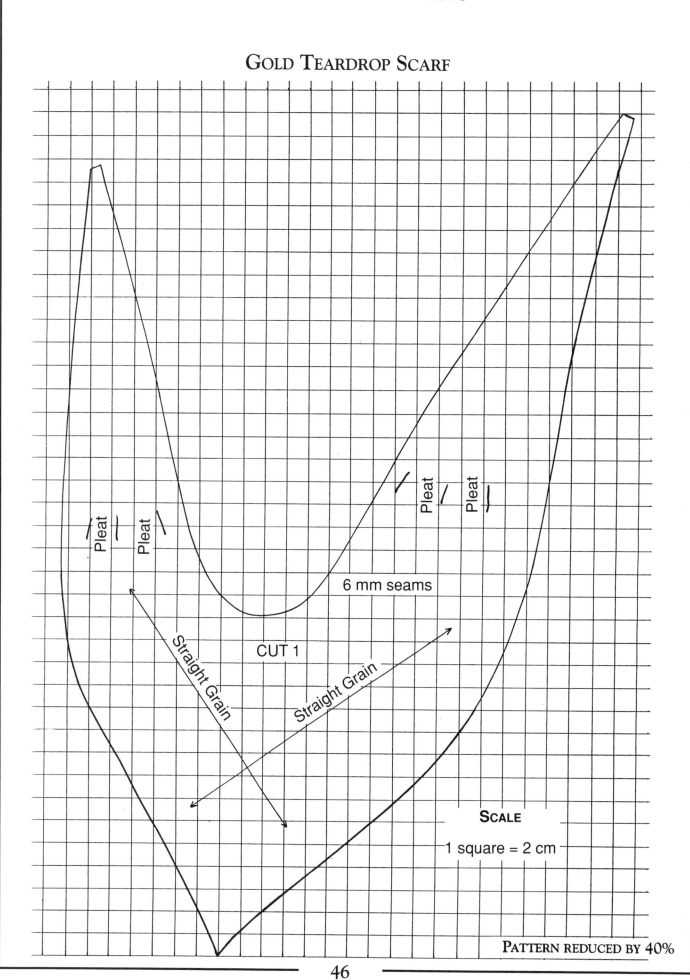

Pleat

Pleat

Pleat

Pleat

6 mm seams

Straight Grain

CUT 1

Straight Grain

SCALE

1 square = 2 cm

PATTERN REDUCED BY 40%

GLASSES CASE AND BOOK COVER

TIP: Choose fabric that will not crush.

REQUIREMENTS

BOOK COVER   25 cm x 36 cm (9¾" x 14¼") fabric
25 cm x 30 cm (9¾" x 12") lining fabric
25 cm x 36 cm (9¾" x 14¼")
Whisperweft® (fusible woven interfacing)

GLASSES CASE   12 cm x 40 cm (4¾" x 15¾") fabric (may
be the same fabric as for the cover)
12 cm x 40 cm (4¾" x 15¾") of lining
fabric (may be the same fabric)
12 cm x 40 cm (4¾" x 15¾") fine iron-on
pellum (if unavailable you may use non
iron-on)

BEADS

2 x 6 mm (¼") dress stones
1 x 5 g (¼ oz) packet small seed beads in pink
1 x 5 g (¼ oz) packet small seed beads in plum
7 x 4 mm (⅛ oz) centre beads in plum
1 x 3 g (⅛ oz) packet clear pink sequins
Small quantity of silver and olive green beads
Matching thread

PREPARATION – BOOK COVER:

● Cut out fabric, lining and Whisperweft® according to
pattern instructions.
● Fuse the Whisperweft® onto the wrong side of the
fabric. Overlock short ends only on both the fabric and
the lining.

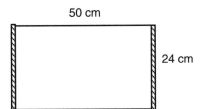

50 cm

24 cm

● Mark the fold lines on the fabric and the centre line on
the section to be beaded. Transfer the design onto the
fabric using one of the methods on page 6. Proceed to
beading instructions.

PREPARATION – GLASSES CASE

● Cut out fabric, lining and iron-on pellum as per pattern instructions. Fuse the pellum to the wrong side of the fabric. Make sure you have the pellum evenly in from the edge of the fabric.

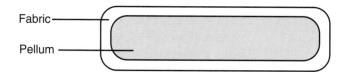

Fabric

Pellum

If you wish to use non iron-on pellum, you will need to baste the pellum in position.

● Place the fabric and lining right sides facing and baste together. Sew around the edge, leaving an opening for turning. Remove basting stitches.

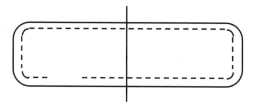

● Clip and trim the seams. Turn to the right side and press. Mark the fold line and the centre of the section to be beaded. Transfer the design using one of the methods on page 6.

BEADING INSTRUCTIONS:

● Begin beading by sewing the dress stone onto the centre of the flower at position Ⓐ on the design sheet.
● Around this bead are six 'cluster' beads. They only go around the lower edge as marked. You can use larger beads for the book cover and small ones for the glasses case.
● The top petals Ⓑ are done as follows.

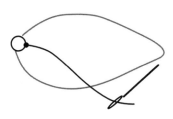

- Begin close to the centre bead in the middle of the petal.
- Thread up eight or 10 beads (eight for small flower, 10 for the larger one). Place them on the fabric and put the needle back into the fabric one bead back from the end. This gives a slightly looped row of beads.

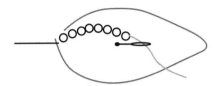

- Bring the needle out in position where the next row is to go.
- Work in this way, looping the beads from the base of the petal to the tip.

TIP: Follow the photograph and design sheet for exact placement of your loops.

- The lower petals ⓒ are edged with seed beads, three at a time. Turn corners so that you have a group of three beads as the point. The glasses case flower petals may be only two beads at a time.
- The two arched arms ⓓ of this flower are filled in with sequin spotting. Overlap sequins to give you the correct shape where necessary.
- The central stamen is single seed spotting. You may need to change the colour of the thread for these, as light-coloured thread may show up too much. The water lines may be either single seeds, one at a time, or, as on the glasses case, loops of beads. If choosing to do the loops, make sure you end off each one before going on to the next.

TO MAKE UP BOOK COVER

- Remove all traces of blue pen or chalk. Allow to dry.
- Fold in the 'lap' ends right sides together. Pin in place.

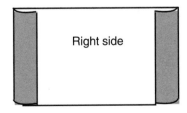

Right side

● Lay the lining over the fabric right sides together.

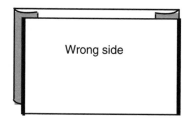

● Stitch along the raw edges (top and bottom) only.

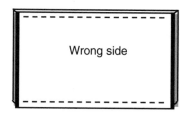

● Turn to the right side and press these seams flat.

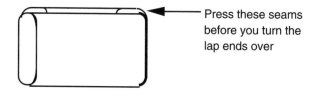

Press these seams
before you turn the
lap ends over

● Now turn the lap ends to the right side and carefully press. DO NOT PRESS THE BEADING!

TO COMPLETE THE GLASSES CASE:

● Remove all traces of blue pen or chalk. Allow to dry.
● Fold along marked line.
● Use ladder stitch or slip stitch to join the two sides. Secure the top of the seam well, as this will need to be strong.
● Press the bottom edge carefully.

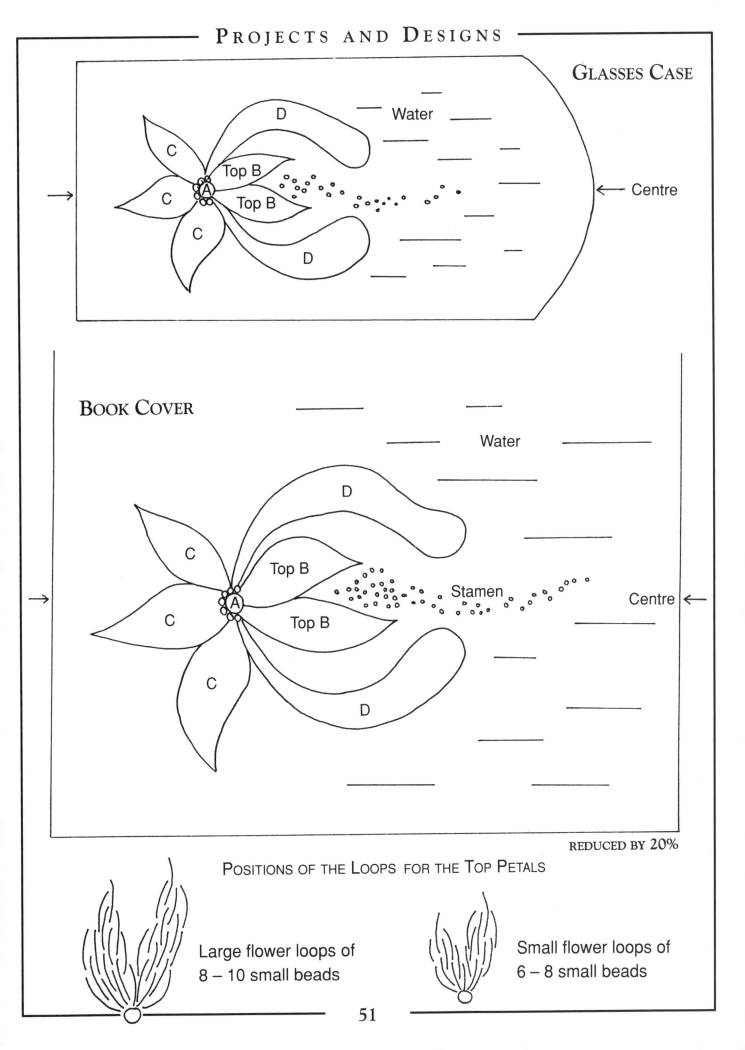

GLASSES CASE

D

C

Top B

A

C

Water

Centre

C

Top B

D

BOOK COVER

Water

D

C

Top B

A

Stamen

Centre

C

Top B

C

D

C

REDUCED BY 20%

POSITIONS OF THE LOOPS FOR THE TOP PETALS

Large flower loops of
8 – 10 small beads

Small flower loops of
6 – 8 small beads

51

BOOK COVER AND GLASSES CASE

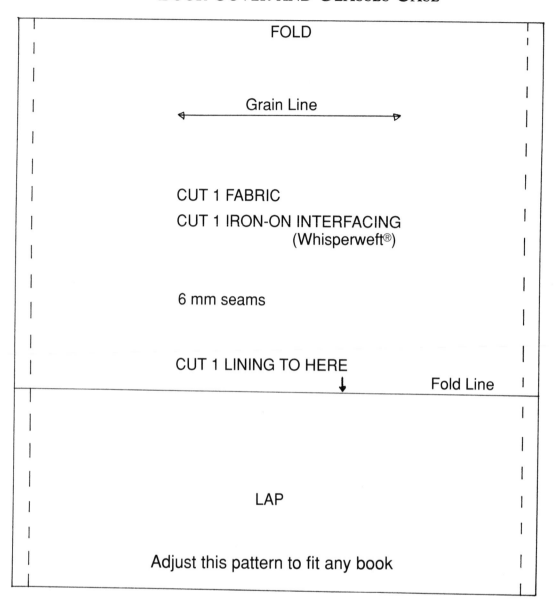

FOLD

Grain Line

CUT 1 FABRIC

CUT 1 IRON-ON INTERFACING
(Whisperweft®)

6 mm seams

CUT 1 LINING TO HERE
↓

Fold Line

LAP

Adjust this pattern to fit any book

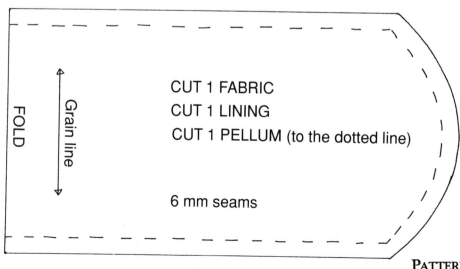

FOLD

Grain line

CUT 1 FABRIC

CUT 1 LINING

CUT 1 PELLUM (to the dotted line)

6 mm seams

PATTERN REDUCED BY 40%

NEEDLE CASE AND PIN CUSHION

REQUIREMENTS

15 cm x 90 cm (6" x 35½") velvet
20 cm x 20 cm (8" x 8") doctor flannel
Small amount of wadding
1.5 m (59") braid, ribbon, or ribbon floss x 2 mm (⅛") wide

BEADS

1 x 5 g (¼ oz) packet small seed beads
30 small (4 mm [⅛"]) bi-cone drop beads
2 x 4 mm (⅛") cut centre beads
(or you can use all the same shape)

PREPARATION OF THE NEEDLE CASE FOR
BEADING

● Trace the needle case pattern. Cut four from velvet.
  Please follow the instructions on the pattern.
● Cut four shapes from the doctor flannel, 1 cm (⅜")
  smaller all around.
● Place two pieces of velvet right sides together and sew
  around the edge using a 6 mm (¼") seam allowance,
  leaving an opening where shown for turning. Repeat for
  the remaining two velvet pieces. These become the
  back and front. See the second diagram.
● Slip stitch or ladder stitch the openings closed and
  press, using a pressing cloth.
● Cut 4 x 18 cm (7") lengths of ribbon.
● Lay these ribbons along the placement lines on the
  front, leaving at least 2 cm (¾") overhanging at the
  front edge.
● Tack in place.

Proceed to beading instructions.

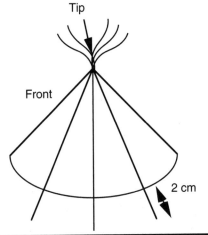

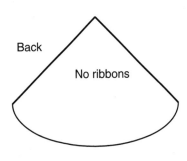

PREPARATION OF PIN CUSHION FOR BEADING

- Trace the pin cushion pattern. Cut two shapes from velvet. Please follow the instructions on the pattern.
- Place these two shapes right sides together and stitch around the edge, using a 6 mm (¼") seam allowance. Leave an opening for turning where shown on the pattern.

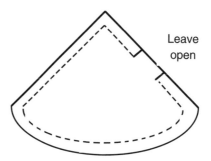

Leave open

- Turn to the right side and press, using a pressing cloth.
- Firmly stuff the pin cushion with wadding. Slip or ladder stitch the opening closed.
- Cut 4 x 18 cm (7") lengths of ribbon.
- Lay these ribbons along the placement lines, leaving at least 2 cm (¾") overhang at the front edge. Tack in place (see diagram above).

Proceed to beading instructions.

BEADING INSTRUCTIONS

- Begin beading over the ribbon, working row 1 towards you from the tip of the fan to the front edge, using three beads at a time.

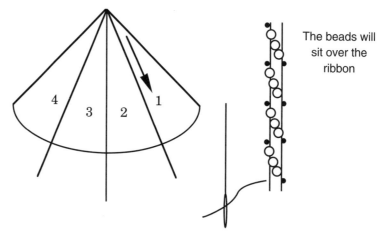

The beads will sit over the ribbon

- Row 4 is beaded away from you, beginning at the tip.

● Rows 2 and 3 are done by attaching a bead approximately every 7 mm (¼") down the centre of the ribbon using a whip stitch.

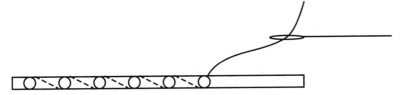

● The dotted line represents the thread on the wrong side of the fabric.

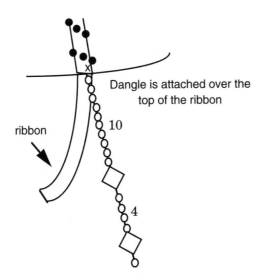

Dangle is attached over the top of the ribbon

ribbon

10

4

● At the end of each row, attach a dangle.
● Sew loops of beads across the rows at the top of the fan. This is row 5 on the pattern. The number of beads you need will depend on the exact size you are using.
● Attach three dangles from the tip of the fan like this:

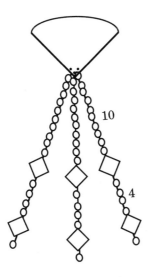

10

4

● Attach your charm over the top of the dangle at the tip. Use a cut centre bead and one small seed bead to anchor it.

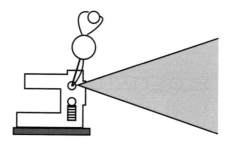

● The charm will cover the support stitches at the base of the dangles.
● Dot the ribbon close to the dangles with FrayStoppa or Fray Check. Allow this to dry completely, then trim the ends as neatly as possible.
● Remove the tacking threads.

TO ASSEMBLE THE NEEDLE CASE

● Sew your four 'pages' of doctor flannel to the back of the needle case between the row 5 line and the tip.

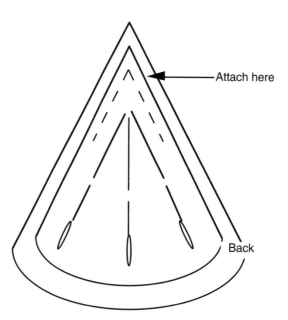

Attach here

Back

● Attach the front to the back in the same position, using a slip stitch or ladder stitch.

This needle case shape is very practical as the points of your needles fit into the tip section. When you pick up the needle case you are less likely to jab your fingers!

NEEDLECASE AND PIN CUSHION

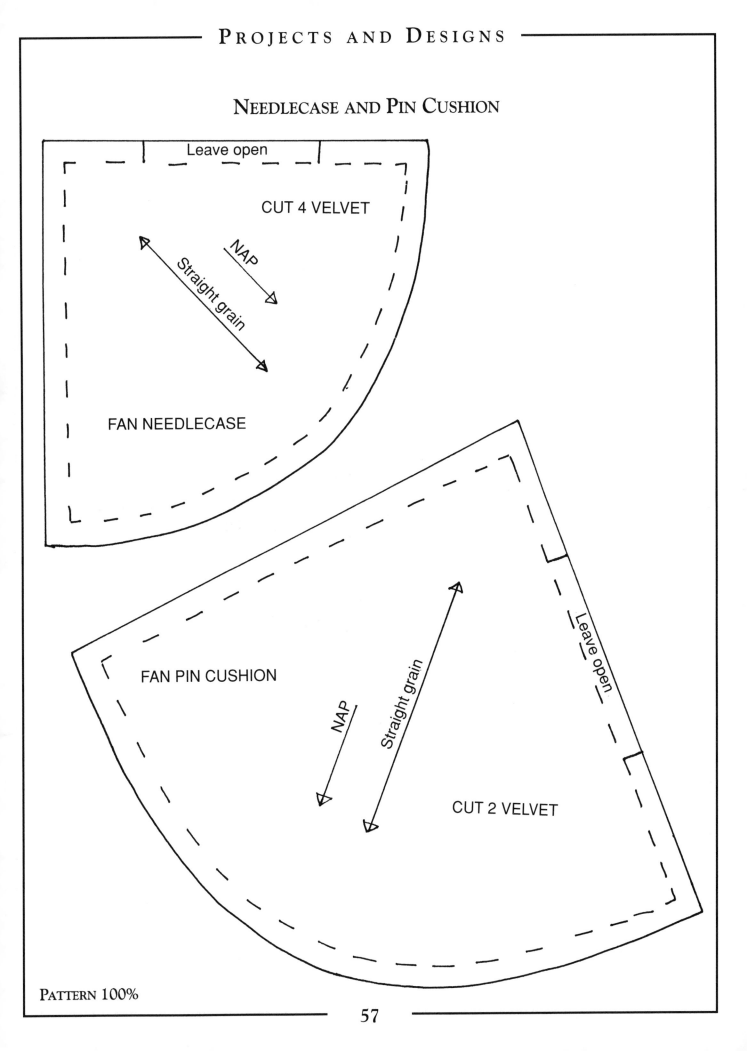

Leave open

CUT 4 VELVET

NAP

Straight grain

FAN NEEDLECASE

FAN PIN CUSHION

NAP

Straight grain

Leave open

CUT 2 VELVET

PATTERN 100%

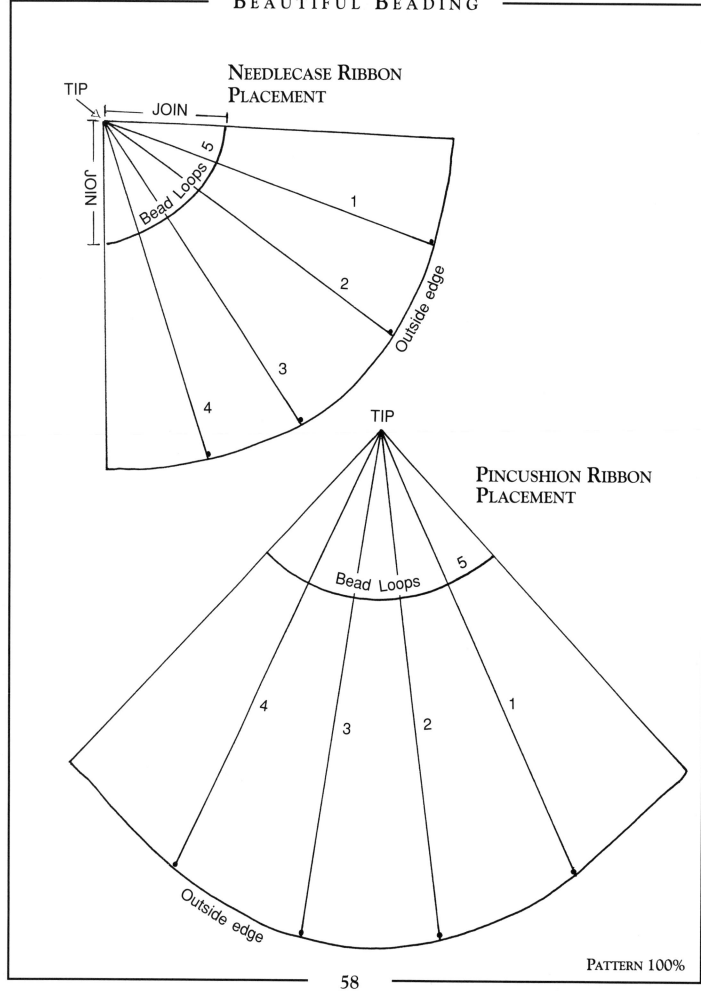

NEEDLECASE RIBBON
PLACEMENT

TIP

JOIN

JOIN

5

Bead Loops

1

2

3

4

Outside edge

TIP

PINCUSHION RIBBON
PLACEMENT

5

Bead Loops

4

3

2

1

Outside edge

PATTERN 100%

SEQUIN FISH

These little fish use only small quantities of beads and sequins; I have used size 5 mm (¼") sequins but 6 mm (⅛") would also be suitable. In addition, you will need one large black seed bead and one silver sequin for the eyes. Choose a fabric which will look like water - painted silk is ideal.

PREPARATION FOR BEADING

- For fine fabrics, press iron-on interfacing, e.g. Whisperweft®, onto the wrong side.
- Transfer the design onto the fabric using one of the methods on page 6.

FISH No 1
- The outline is done first using seed beads one at a time.

TIP: To get these tiny beads in a straight line, take tiny stitches from right to left.

- The inside body section is filled in with sequins one at a time. Follow the direction of the arrows on the design sheet.
- The eye on this fish is a single chunky black bead. Sew this on with a single back stitch.
- The tail is made by bringing the thread up at the beginning of a line (marked on the design). Take a support stitch. Thread onto the needle four seeds, one sequin, one seed, one sequin, one seed, one sequin, one seed, one sequin, one seed, one sequin – total of 13 on the needle together. Take a stitch out from the beginning the length of the line and pass the needle through to the back. Secure at the back and then go straight to the next row. Continue with this until all rows are filled in.

FISH No 2
- The outline for the body is done using seed beads one at a time.
- The body sections are filled in using sequins one at a time. Change colours and work in the direction of the arrows on the design sheet.
- The eye is sewn on using a silver sequin and one black chunky seed bead. This is sewn in the same way as for sequin spotting.
- The tail is sewn using loops of tiny seed beads in a contrast colour. Follow the lines on the design sheet.
- Fill in around the eye with seed spotting.

FISH No 3
- The outline of the body is done with small seeds one at a time.
- The eye is sewn on using a silver sequin and one black chunky seed bead, as for sequin spotting.
- The body is filled in completely with sequins one at a time. Mix the colours up as you go.

FISH No 4
(Slightly harder than the other fish)
This fish has no beaded edge, so keeping the sequins straight is very important. Remember to take the stitch exactly on the line you have drawn. If you do this you should have no problems.

- Begin with thread to match the dark sequins on the face. Sew the sequins on from the top of the mouth over the head, then end off and begin again on the next row.

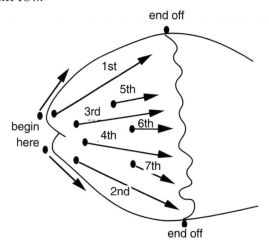

- Work each row like this until all the spaces are filled. Remember that you should just be able to see the hole in the sequin but not the thread. The first sequin thread is the only one visible.
- Next sew on the eye over the top of the filled-in face section. I have used a black centre bead for the eye and a dark blue sequin. Sew these on the same way as for sequin spotting.
- Now change the thread colour to match the sequins on the body. Work the same way as the face, following the body line to the tail.
- Fill in the body completely with different coloured sequins.
- The tail on this fish is done using ordinary sequins and sequins with a hole to one side. Begin in the centre and work out to the edges. Thread together four seed

beads, one sequin, one chunky bead, one sequin, one chunky bead, one flat sequin, one chunky bead, one flat sequin, one chunky bead, one sequin, one chunky bead and one flat sequin – a total of 15 on your needle. The stitch out is the length of the line on the design. Secure this at the back before going onto the next row. Bead each of the longest rows first, then omit one bead and one sequin for each of the shorter rows. This makes a beautiful tail!

● The lower fin is first beaded like a dangle, then caught in place through the last bead after all the lines are beaded.

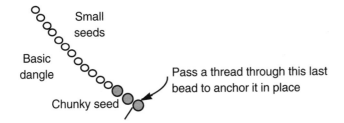

● Thread up beads to the same length as the line.
● The upper fin is done in the same way.

See how many other different ways you can do these little fish, or design some of your own!

WEEDS AND SEA URCHIN

If you want to create an underwater scene, I have beaded weeds and a sea creature which I hope looks like an urchin.

WEEDS
● To bead the weeds, sew the first row three beads at a time working away from yourself, up the row.

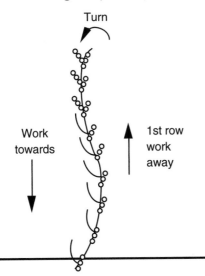

● Turn at the top and begin the next set to alternate with the first. Line these beads up with the middle bead of the group. They will curve around the previous row. This is a variation of the feather stitch.

SEA URCHIN
● Draw this where you want to place your urchin:

● Sew a few seed beads in the circle.
● Fill in the spaces with single bugle bead and double bugle bead clusters.
● The arms are beaded in the same way as a central large flower, but add an extra bead and sequin for the three longest rows.

You could also add a starfish by beading a small spider flower.

TO MOUNT YOUR FISH INSIDE A TIMBER BOX LID:

REQUIREMENTS:

Fine wadding, craft glue.

● Select a box the correct size to suit the fish you have beaded.
● Cut a small piece of fine wadding the same size as the inside of the frame lid.
● Position the frame lid over your beaded fabric and mark the outside edge. Cut along this line.

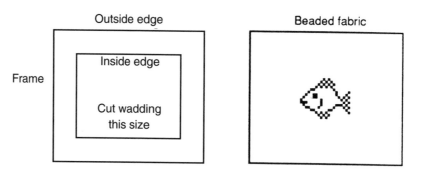

● Glue the wadding shape in the centre of the backing board.

Backing board

Wadding

Dot with glue

- Dot craft glue around the wadding on the backing board only.
- Lay the beaded fabric right side up over the wadding. Be very careful to keep your fabric flat over the wadding.

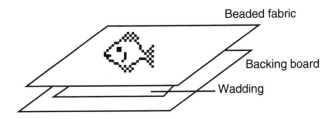

Beaded fabric

Backing board

Wadding

- Trim the fabric to the same size as the backing board.
- Check to make sure the design is positioned correctly for the frame.
- Dot glue around the edge of the fabric within the frame line, not on the padded fabric.
- Fit your fabric-covered board inside your frame lid and LEAVE TO DRY!

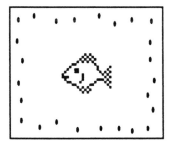

These boxes come in various sizes and are also available round as well as square and rectangle. The little fish can also be framed or put in the lid of a glass crystal jar. Why not bead a few onto a top?

SEQUIN FISH

1

2

3

4

EVENING JACKET

This jacket has been worked mainly in black cut beads. The bag has more silver added to show how the addition of a contrast changes the look of a design. This design would also look great in gold beads on cream fabric.

REQUIREMENTS:

Pattern and fabric for a jacket (I chose a bolero style with a set-in sleeve)
Whisperweft® (or fine woven iron-on interfacing) – enough to cover the front and back of your jacket completely
Thread to match the jacket

BEADS:

2 large oval dress stones at least 1.2 cm (½") long
2 oval dress stones 2 cm (¾") long
12 cut glass centres
4 x 5 g (¼ oz) packets cut seed beads
1 x 5 g (¼ oz) packet cut contrast seed beads
1 x 5 g (¼ oz) packet size 2 bugle beads
2 x 3 g (⅛ oz) packets sequins
24 drop beads
1 x 5 g (¼ oz) packet rice beads

PREPARATION OF YOUR JACKET FOR BEADING:

● Cut out your jacket according to the pattern.
● Also cut out the front and back sections in Whisperweft®.
● Fuse the Whisperweft® onto the wrong side of both fronts and the back.

NB: Whisperweft® must be used according to the manufacturer's instructions for best results.

● Sew together the shoulder seams on the jacket. Press seams flat.
● Follow instructions for preparing a garment for beading on page 6, omitting the section about backing as you already have the Whisperweft® on. TRY IT ON before you transfer the design.

NB: The shoulder spray position must be accurate as the dangle and large oval bead are a feature of the design.

Make sure the oval bead is going to sit at the top of the shoulder and is not too close to the sleeve seam – 2 cm (¾") is enough room for the sewing machine foot to fit past. If you have trouble, sew the top section of the sleeve using the zipper foot attachment on your sewing machine.

BEADING INSTRUCTIONS:

● The shoulder spray is worked first. Place the large oval bead in position and sew it on using a seed bead to cover the hole, as in the Oriental Pouch Bag instructions, page 74.

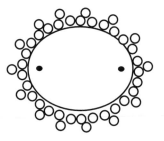

● Work a single bugle bead cluster around this oval bead. Follow the diagram for the position of the beads. Get them as close as possible to each other and the oval bead.
● The radiating arms are sewn next. Follow the design sheet for the direction of beading and the row numbers.
● Rows 1, 3, 5, 6, 8 and 10 are sewn using three seed beads, one sequin, one bead and one sequin.
● Rows 2, 4, 7 and 9 are sewn using three beads at a time.
● The rows with beads and sequins finish with single seed spotting in a contrast colour.
● The rows with three beads at a time finish with a central bead with contrast seed beads around it. Follow the design sheet for the placement.
● Sprinkle seed spotting in between the two sections of sprays.
● Repeat this for the lower front sprays, using the smaller oval dress stones. Follow the design sheet for beading directions for each side.
● When you have completed beading on both shoulders and the two front panels, assemble the jacket following the pattern instructions. Press carefully.

DO NOT PRESS SEQUINS, AS THEY WILL FLATTEN!

● The shoulder dangles are worked from the centre out on each side and hang from beside the bugle bead cluster, surrounding the large oval bead on the shoulder point.

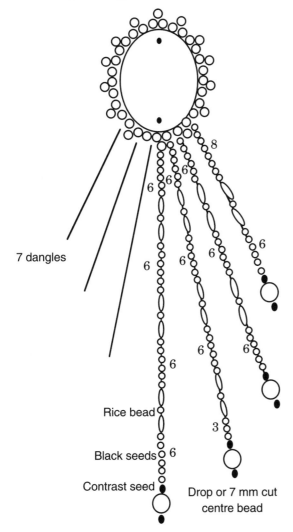

7 dangles

Rice bead

Black seeds 6

Contrast seed

Drop or 7 mm cut centre bead

This is the order I have used, but you can use bugle beads or cut centres instead of rice beads if you prefer.

● Follow the directions for a basic dangle. Note that these are far longer than your needle so that the thread back through as far as you can the first time, then pass the needle through the rest of the dangle. Some patience is needed with this. Remember not to let go of the seed bead at the end (your anchor) until you have the thread completely through all the beads.

Hold this bead firmly

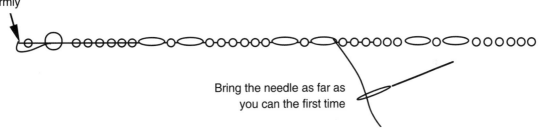

Bring the needle as far as you can the first time

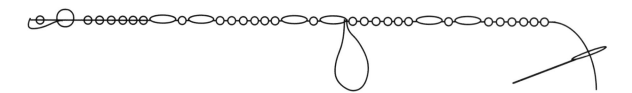

- If you have trouble managing this long dangle, do short ones!
- The front dangles are worked from beside the bugle bead cluster on the lower edge of the oval dress stone.

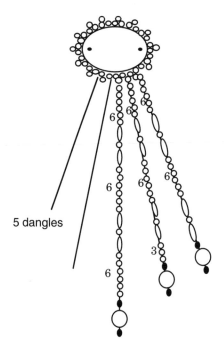

5 dangles

- Work them in the same way as the basic dangles for the shoulder.

The jacket I made also has a small stone at the wrist, but this is optional.

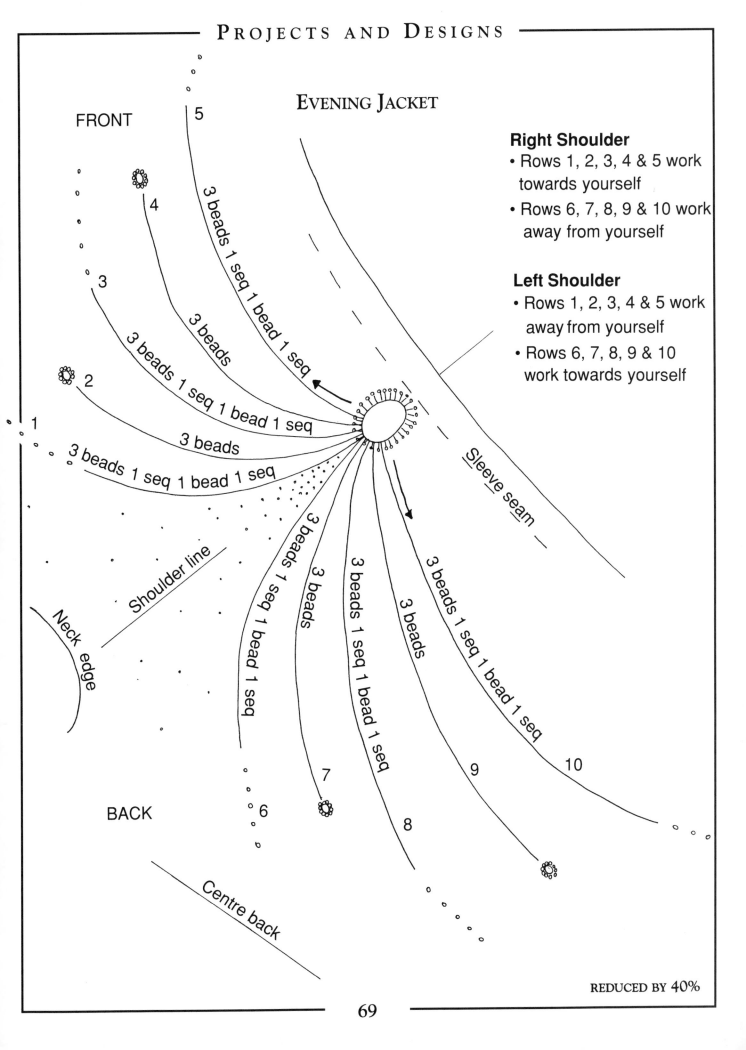

EVENING JACKET

FRONT

5

3 beads 1 seq 1 bead 1 seq

4

3 beads

3

3 beads 1 seq 1 bead 1 seq

2

3 beads

3 beads 1 seq 1 bead 1 seq

1

Right Shoulder
- Rows 1, 2, 3, 4 & 5 work towards yourself
- Rows 6, 7, 8, 9 & 10 work away from yourself

Left Shoulder
- Rows 1, 2, 3, 4 & 5 work away from yourself
- Rows 6, 7, 8, 9 & 10 work towards yourself

Sleeve seam

Shoulder line

Neck edge

3 beads 1 seq 1 bead 1 seq

3 beads

3 beads 1 seq 1 bead 1 seq

3 beads

3 beads 1 seq 1 bead 1 seq

BACK

6

7

8

9

10

Centre back

REDUCED BY 40%

EVENING JACKET

Right Hand Side Front

• Work all rows away
  from yourself

Left Hand Side Front

• Work all rows
  towards yourself

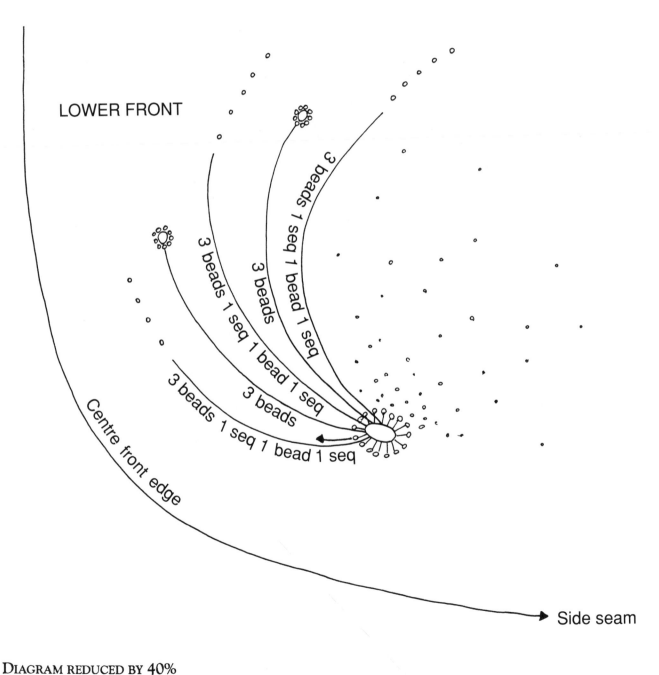

LOWER FRONT

3 beads 1 seq 1 bead 1 seq

3 beads

3 beads 1 seq 1 bead 1 seq

3 beads

3 beads 1 seq 1 bead 1 seq

Centre front edge

Side seam

EVENING BAG

REQUIREMENTS

30 cm x 50 cm (11¾" x 19¾") fabric for the purse
30 cm x 50 cm (11¾" x 19¾") iron-on pellum or fine
wadding
30 cm x 50 cm (11¾" x 19¾") satin lining to match
Thread to match the fabric

BEADS
1 oval dress stone 12 mm (⅜") long
1 packet bugle beads size 2
A small amount of silver beads
1 packet sequins
1 packet small cut seed beads
Size 1 bugle beads or chunky beads for the edging,
optional

PREPARATION OF THE BAG FOR BEADING

● Enlarge the pattern shape on page 73.
● Cut one pattern from the fabric and one from lining.
● Cut one pattern from the pellum and trim off 1 cm
  (⅜") all round.
● Fuse the smaller pellum to the wrong side of the fabric.
● Transfer the design onto the right side of the fabric in
  the position indicated. Use one of the methods
  described on page 6.

BEADING INSTRUCTIONS

Follow the instructions for beading on the jacket,
omitting the dangle.

TO CONSTRUCT THE BAG

● Lay the lining and beaded fabric right sides together.
  Pin and tack in place.

● Stitch around the edge using a 1 cm (³⁄₈") seam allowance, leaving the short straight end open for turning.

Leave open

● Trim and clip the seam.
● Turn to the right side and press the edges only. Be very careful not to press your beading.
● Stitch the opening closed using either a ladder stitch or slip stitch.
● Fold the bag where shown on the pattern. Press carefully. Slip stitch or ladder stitch the two sides of the bag.

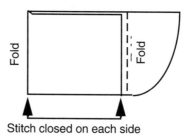

Fold

Fold

Stitch closed on each side

Beaded edging of your choice may be done along the curved edge. Instructions for edging can be found on page 30. The bag photographed has a single seed edge using size 1 bugle bead and then a silver seed bead.

EVENING BAG

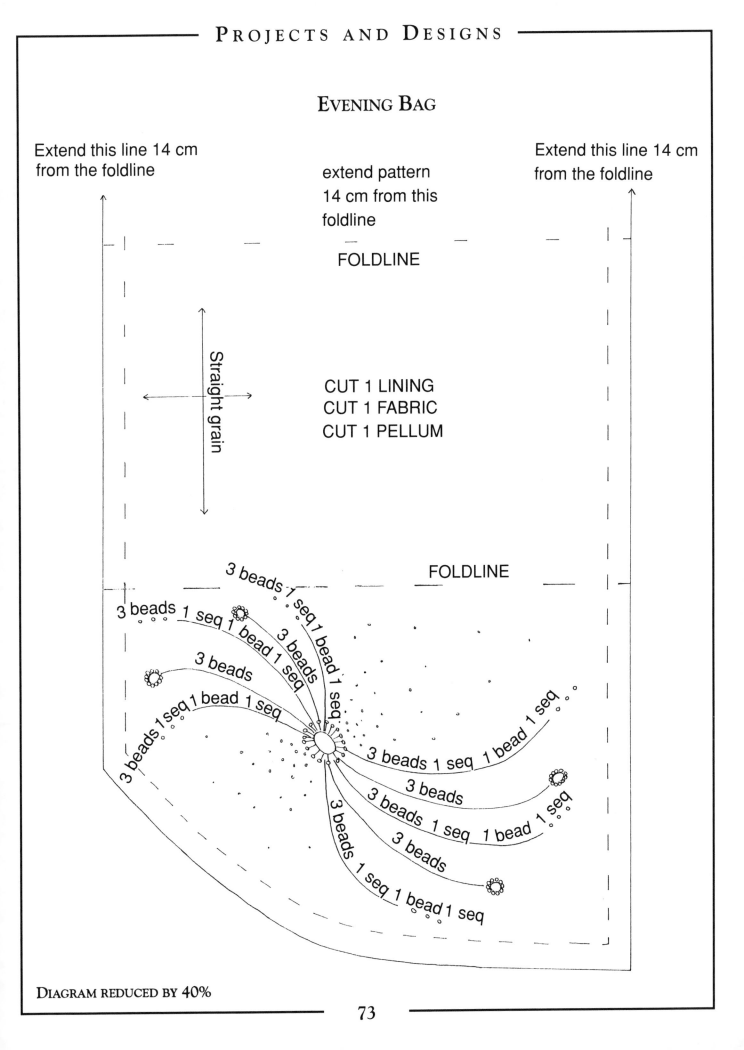

Extend this line 14 cm from the foldline

extend pattern 14 cm from this foldline

Extend this line 14 cm from the foldline

FOLDLINE

Straight grain

CUT 1 LINING
CUT 1 FABRIC
CUT 1 PELLUM

FOLDLINE

3 beads 1 seq 1 bead 1 seq

3 beads 1 seq 1 bead 1 seq

3 beads

3 beads

3 beads 1 seq 1 bead 1 seq

3 beads 1 seq 1 bead 1 seq

3 beads

3 beads 1 seq 1 bead 1 seq

3 beads

3 beads 1 seq 1 bead 1 seq

DIAGRAM REDUCED BY 40%

ORIENTAL POUCH BAG

REQUIREMENTS

35 cm x 35 cm (13¾" x 13¾") square plain fabric
35 cm x 35 cm (13¾" x 13¾") square printed fabric
35 cm x 70 cm (13¾" x 27½") piece organza
Thread to match the fabrics
32 x silver or gold rings large enough to fit two thicknesses of your drawstring cords through easily (jump rings)
1.5 m (59") cord, 3-4 mm (⅛") thick (I have used three very narrow cords, plaited together to form one 4 mm [⅛"] cord)
1 plastic ice cream container lid

BEADS

4 x 1.2 cm (½") oval dress stones
12 x 6 mm (¼") faceted crystal or bi-cone beads (optional)
1 x 5 g (¼oz) packet size 2 bugle beads
2 x 5 g (¼oz) packet chunky beads (I used size 1 bugle bead as my chunky beads)
1 x 5 g (¼oz) packet small seed beads in a contrasting colour
1 x 3 g (⅛oz) packet sequins

NOTE: When cutting out your squares, make sure you have them exactly on the straight grain and cut accurately.

PREPARING THE BAG FOR BEADING

- Cut 2 x 30.5 cm (13¾") squares from the organza.
- Cut 1 x 30.5 cm (13¾") square from the plain and printed fabrics.
- Cut 1 x 10 cm (4") diameter circle from the plastic ice cream container lid.
- Mark the centre on the plastic circle and the two organza squares.
- Place the plastic in between these two organza squares, matching the centres. Pin and tack around the plastic to keep it in place.

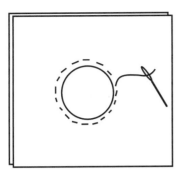
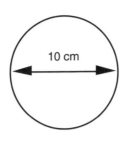

10 cm

- Tack the two outside edges of the squares together.
- Place the plain and printed squares right sides together. Then place the organza squares over the plain fabric.

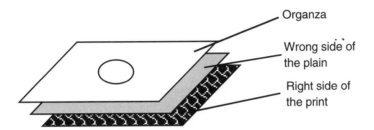

Organza

Wrong side of the plain

Right side of the print

- Pin and tack the squares together.
- Using a 6 mm (¼") seam width, sew neatly around the outside of the squares with a fine straight stitch on your sewing machine. Make sure you leave a 10 cm (4") opening on one side.

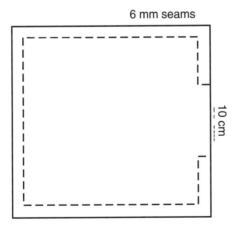

6 mm seams

10 cm

- Clip the corners and turn to the right side. Press carefully. Make sure the sides of the square are even (they should be exactly 29 cm [11½"] long) and that the corners have nice points. The dangles will fall from the corners so you don't want to have any lumps and bumps there!
- Slip stitch or ladder stitch the opening closed.

You are now ready to begin beading.

BEADING INSTRUCTIONS

● The edging is done first. I have used a single bead edge, but you can also use the cluster edge. It does take more beads though, so make sure you have enough. Edging instructions are on page 30.

● Measure 8.5 cm (3⅜") from each corner and then mark your diagonal fold line cross (see pattern diagram). Mark the placement of the rings 3 cm (1¼") apart.

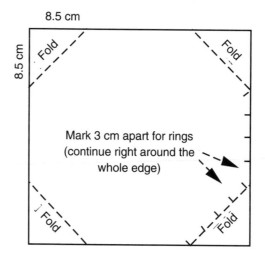

Mark 3 cm apart for rings
(continue right around the
whole edge)

● Mark the design onto each corner section, using an organza tracing as explained on page 6. Make sure you have it exactly in the centre of the corner triangle.
● Sew the centre oval bead in position for the flower. It is best to use a small seed bead to cover the hole on the large bead like this.

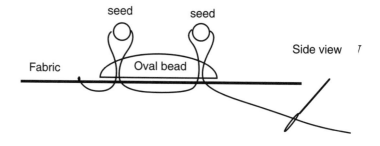

The seed bead forms an anchor to hold the bead down.

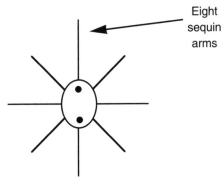

Eight
sequin
arms

● Use this plan to form your flower. The sequin arms are
sewn on in the same way as for the central large flower
on page 19. Use one small seed, one chunky seed, one
small seed, one sequin, one chunky seed, one sequin,
one chunky seed, one sequin.

● Fill in the spaces between the sequin arms with loops of
4 chunky seeds and one small contrast seed bead.

● Sew the bugle beads in place using a back stitch, as
explained on page 12.
● Sew single seed spotting where marked.
● Repeat this flower on each of the four corner triangles.
● Sew the rings in positions as marked.

DANGLES

The middle dangle is done first, then the two either side.
Take a small support stitch at the back of the corner
point, close to the edging. Form the dangles as follows.

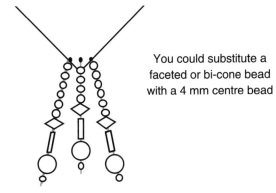

You could substitute a
faceted or bi-cone bead
with a 4 mm centre bead

Repeat at each corner point.

- Cut 2 x 55 cm (21¾") lengths of cord. Thread the cord for the drawstring as follows.

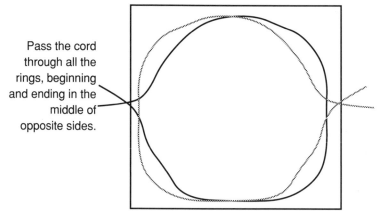

Pass the cord through all the rings, beginning and ending in the middle of opposite sides.

- Knot both ends together at each side position. A dangle may be sewn through the knots to match the dangles at the corners.

NOTE: Pull the drawstrings carefully when closing your bag.

This bag may be made in different sizes. Just use a larger or smaller square and adjust the ring positions accordingly.

ORIENTAL POUCH

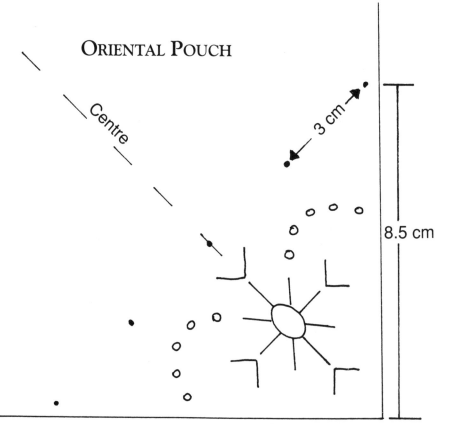

Centre

3 cm

8.5 cm

Finished edge of the bag

FLOWER BELT

REQUIREMENTS

20 cm x 115 cm (8" x 45¼") fabric
20 cm x 60 cm (8" x 23½") firm Vilene (iron-on) or
Armoweft® (Armoweft® is like Whisperweft®, only firmer)
30 cm x 2.5 cm (11¾" x 1") wide elastic
1 skirt hook
Thread to match fabric

BEADS:
2 x 5 g (¼ oz) packets mauve seed beads
1 x 5 g (¼ oz) packet silver cut seed beads
1 x 5 g (¼ oz) packet green seed beads
3 x 7 mm (¼") dress stones
7 x 4 mm (⅛") drops or cut centre beads
Small amount of sequins to match the flower

PREPARATION OF THE BELT FOR BEADING

● Enlarge the pattern on page 83.

NOTE: this belt is adjustable and will fit sizes 10-16.

● Cut out one in fabric and cut one from the Armoweft®
  or Vilene.
● Press the Armoweft® onto the wrong side of the fabric.
● Transfer the design onto right side of belt, matching the
  centre marks.
● Check to make sure you have the flower exactly in the
  middle and that both sides of your design are the same.

BEADING INSTRUCTIONS

● Begin with the main flower in the centre of the design.
● Sew one dress stone in place in the middle of the main
  flower.
● Around this stone sew a finger flower. For the silver tips
  on each petal, thread five mauve seeds and three silver
  seeds onto the needle for the last five rows on each
  petal (Nos. 4, 5, 6, 7 and 8).
● Sew dress stones in position for the side flowers and
  work two petals where shown on the design sheet.

- Around the other side of these dress stones, sew a 'cluster' row of beads.

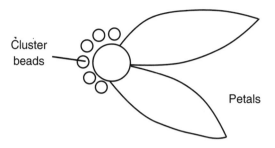

Cluster beads

Petals

- The leaves are loops of green seeds with three silver seeds at the ends.

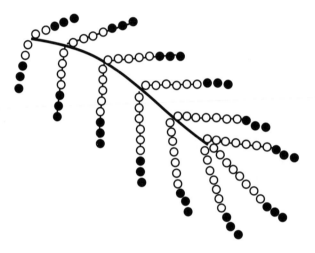

This is a guide for each leaf. Adjust the numbers of beads according to the size of the seed beads you are using.

- Next do the border lines. Work in the direction indicated on the design sheet. I have used three seed beads at a time, or you could use a bugle bead and seed bead.
- At the end of each of these rows, I have sewn a centre bead with seeds around.
- Beside each of the rows of three seeds, I have sewn a row of single seeds, spaced to match each group of three seeds.

● The last step is to sew three dangles on the main flower. These dangles fall from in between the lower petals (X).

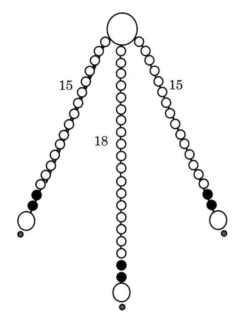

● Beads I have used for my basic dangles are as follows:

TO FINISH YOUR BELT

● Wash all traces of blue pen or chalk from your fabric using clean water.
● Cut an 8 cm x 9 cm ($3\frac{1}{8}$" x $3\frac{1}{2}$") piece of fabric for the tab. Cut 6 cm ($2\frac{3}{8}$") of 2.5 cm (1") elastic.

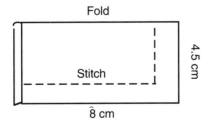

- Fold the tab in half as shown:
- Stitch along the 8 cm (3⅛") edge and across one end using a 12 mm (½") seam allowance.
- Turn to the right side and press.
- Slide the elastic inside this tab and stitch across the opening to hold the elastic in place.
- Tack the tab in place on the belt where marked on the pattern. Sizes 10-12 will only need a short gathered tab. For the other side, cut your elastic to make up your waist measurement. Cut your fabric 9 cm (3½") wide and one and a half times the length of the elastic.
- Repeat the steps for the tab, only this side will be gathered over the elastic.
- Tack this gathered tab in place on the opposite side of the belt:

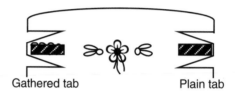

Gathered tab   Plain tab

- Sew the four side darts, making sure that the finished size will be the same as the side tabs. Press.
- Sew the centre back seam using a 1 cm (⅜") seam allowance, leaving an opening for turning as shown on the pattern. Press this seam open carefully - DO NOT press on the sequins.

Leave open

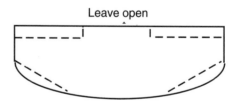

- Turn to the right side, carefully, so you don't damage your beading.
- Slip or ladder stitch the opening closed.
- Sew the skirt hook in position on each end of the tabs.

FLOWER BELT

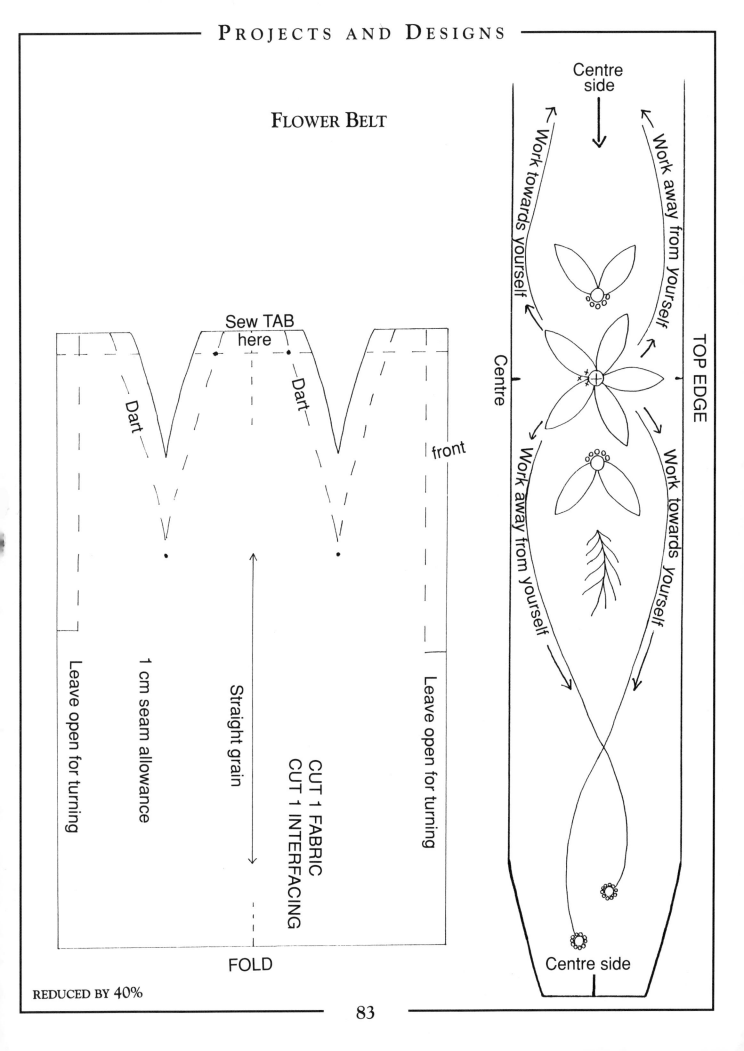

Sew TAB here

Dart

Dart

front

Leave open for turning

1 cm seam allowance

Straight grain

CUT 1 FABRIC
CUT 1 INTERFACING

Leave open for turning

FOLD

REDUCED BY 40%

Centre side

Work away from yourself

Work towards yourself

TOP EDGE

Centre

Work away from yourself

Work towards yourself

Centre side

GLOSSARY OF TERMS USED

Fuse — to adhere or fix to fabric using heat to melt a pre-glued interfacing or wadding.

Grainline — the weave of the fabric running parallel with the selvedge or woven side edge of the fabric.

Ladder stitch — pulled tight this closes to form an invisible join.

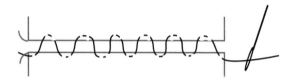

Pellum — fine wadding.

Roll hem — a hem where the raw edge is rolled under. This may be done on an overlocker or machine, or by hand.

Slip stitch — taking a small stitch on either side to join two edges, and make a visible join.

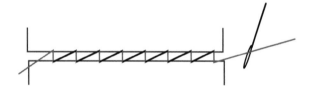

Stay stitch — a row of machine stitching done to stabilise a raw edge.

Support stitch — a small back stitch done to begin, or end off a row of beading.

Tacking — a running stitch done around the edge to hold your fabric in place, OR, small running stitches done in contrast thread to outline a design before beading.

Trim and clip — cutting back the seam to approximately 3 mm wide. Cutting the corner off close to the stitching to reduce the bulk of fabric when turning right side out.

Whip stitch